Testimonials for *The Dream Belongs to the Dreamer*

"My experience was that it was very easy to go through the process and it was straight-forward in finding the primary symbol, and understanding it." Adrian Mcginn, Executive Coach

"If you ever needed help understanding your dreams you never will again. Buy this book, you'll see for yourself." Life Coach Simone Peer, MA, PCC, PMC

"When I used this dream method I found it very easy to get through the process. It was very straightforward and I didn't need any additional help. Any words I came across that needed clarity were immediately explained in the next sentence. I recommend this process to anyone interested in understanding their dreams." Rosemary Jansen Zelazek, RN

"I was an early critical reader of this book. I found the dream method easy to use. The language was not too psycho-babbly and that alone made it easy to negotiate and understand." Sherry Catrell Williamson

"As a caregiver I've learned we heal from the inside out. Once we do we can fully experience the magic of the life God has given us. The Dream Belongs to the Dreamer is a book written expressly for deep healing, the kind of healing we all need to experience to live, love and grow to our fullest potential." Cynthia Brennan, LMSW, Author, "Living, Loving, and Unlearning"

"The Dream Belongs to the Dreamer" is the kind of book you can use as a dream reference over and over again to gain insight into how you tick. Pop it in your bag or purse and refer to it often. It is the first dream book written for the mainstream population, and is destined to become a timeless classic in the self-help field." Wally Ruele, Sedona, AZ

"If you can't explain it simply, you don't understand it well enough." Albert Einstein

"Velva, Thank you so much for your wonderful insight and suggestions about my dream. Yes, I did an active imagination and engaged my dream symbols. Many aha! moments and life happenings revealed. Thanks again for your special brand of expertise." Tishanne Patterson, Dreamer

"Dream Momma, I love reading the stories on your page. Dreams have always fascinated me. Think this will be my favorite FB page. Thank you for sharing!" Debbie Barrett OMary

"Can't wait to read the book!!" Keri Silk, Professional Trainer and Coach

THE DREAM BELONGS TO THE DREAMER

A HANDS-ON, HOW-TO, STEP-BY-STEP GUIDE
TO UNDERSTANDING YOUR DREAMS

VELVA LEE HERATY, MSW

Balboa Press books may be ordered through booksellers or by contacting:

Balboa Press
A Division of Hay House
1663 Liberty Drive
Bloomington, IN 47403
www.balboapress.com
1 (877) 407-4847

Printed in the United States of America.

ISBN: 978-1-4525-8712-7 (sc)
ISBN: 978-1-4525-8711-0 (e)

Library of Congress Control Number: 2013920725

Balboa Press rev. date: 08/11/2014

CONTENTS

PREFACE

We all dream. Many of us spend restless nights tossing and turning over mysterious, provocative dream images and symbols. Images and symbols that can be both intriguing and terrifying. Sometimes we have a BIG dream, a dream that haunts us for months. Other times nightmares hold us in their grip, our hearts pounding. Perhaps we cry out. Some nights we may have a sensuous body dream or a garden-variety dream that rehashes the day's events.

Whatever type of dream we have, most of us are adrift and confused by its impact and meaning. Often we run to a bookstore, go online, or visit a library to look up the symbols, thus giving our precious dream away to a total stranger. After reading this book you'll never be confused by a dream and its meaning again.

INTRODUCTION

Imagine yourself standing on the shore at the edge of a vast sea stretching as far as you can see. You're a busy person with many demands on your time but as you stand there in your quieter moments you wonder how far away the other shore is or does the sea roll on forever? Then one restless day you imagine the far shore. It seems to call to you and something very deep inside of you stirs. It feels like an awakening. You look back and see that nothing has changed but then, once you look forward, the beckoning feels stronger. You begin to pace the shoreline wanting more. More what? The answer isn't clear but the feeling strengthens. Then one day you suddenly realize you need to go to the far shore.

As this need becomes urgent, off in the distance you see a small vessel growing larger as it nears. You eagerly hail it waving both arms and in a few compelling moments your journey to the far shore begins. You never look back.

ABOUT THE AUTHOR

Think of me as one of the many vessels navigating the seas of the unconscious for willing passengers such as yourself. You board, we map your route, you travel along your route and eventually you disembark. It's important that I remain the captain of my small ship, yet it is equally important I share the helm with you if you're willing to share the responsibilities and choices of your journey. My book is dedicated to you. You are among those bold seafarers who ultimately took the route less traveled and made it safely to the far shore. Those adventurers who found their unique, often challenging route to self-identity, or what my theoretical guide Carl Jung would call the True Self. Welcome aboard!

I didn't start out willing to navigate these dark waters, the vast seas that Jung labeled *the collective unconscious.* I started out helping my clients go from point A to B. From drinking to not drinking. From alcoholism to sobriety. My ship then was a large cargo ship that laboriously went from port to port, the journey being the wisdom of the Twelve Steps.

My professional interest in alcoholic family systems was personal so I developed an exploratory research project into the Adult Children of Alcoholics (ACOA) syndrome that 532 people responded to. It was a tremendous learning curve for me and soon after that I began a private practice specializing in ACOA dynamics. During this period a client brought me a dream that challenged both of us and in professional frustration I sought answers at the C. G. Jung Institute in

Evanston, Illinois. Seven years later my professional identity as a Jungian depth-psychotherapist with dream expertise was realized.

At the C. G. Jung Institute, a well-recognized hotbed of Jungian training, I enrolled in a course on dreams led by Dr. Murray Stein and Dr. James Wylie, two extraordinary clinicians and trainers. Stein became my mentor and as of this writing is a training analyst at the International School for Analytical Psychology in Zurich, Switzerland.

While there I read all of Jung, most of James Hillman, and dozens of other Jungian theorists and authors. I attended many classes and conferences and slowly felt my clinical approach shift from the cognitive-behavioral model best suited for alcoholic recovery to Jungian depth-psychotherapy, a deeper quest for the True Self.

Once I applied the power of dreamwork in my practice, wondrous things happened. Clients made deeper commitments to the process and gained a level of self-understanding more quickly. Core wounds from the unconscious were revealed, processed, and integrated, often when we thought our therapeutic work was coming to an end. I witnessed mastery over what in the past was considered insurmountable by many clinical theorists. It was then that my clinical practice became more collaborative and I was no longer the sole helmsman. My clients stayed longer in therapy and accomplished such a deep healing that they were truly whole when our work was done. To this day I see those clients who went the distance to self-discovery as heroes of their own journeys and monuments to the power of commitment, resiliency, and personal growth. I will never forget them.

This client collaboration led to another milestone in my

professional career. Through it I developed a dream processing method that was not only powerful but user-friendly and efficient too. I named this process the Subjective Symbol Immersion Method or SSIM. Over time I refined it and began teaching SSIM to fellow clinicians and lay people alike since it didn't rely on confusing clinical terminology or what is commonly called "psycho-babble." You will learn and master it while reading *The Dream Belongs to the Dreamer.*

Eventually I brought SSIM to the University of Chicago School of Social Work, Columbia College and DePaul University. Then to conferences in Norway and on the invitation of Bjorn Brittannia, to Iceland. The National Wellness Association asked me to create a child's version of SSIM and a workbook was born designed to help children three years old and up conquer the fears that trigger nightmares. Loyola Academy in Wilmette brought me in to introduce SSIM to their Senior Honors Class and it was interesting to see how creatively they used my method. I have also taught SSIM in St. Petersburg, Florida where retirees and seniors gathered to share their dreams and dream symbols. I even taught SSIM on a cruise ship crossing the Atlantic Ocean. Everywhere I went, SSIM went too. From these experiences I learned it was not only for everybody, it was for all ages and all places too.

As I look back I am moved by my alcoholic clients and their journeys to sobriety and beyond to personal growth. I understood they were dealing with a life-threatening illness, that alcoholism is a fatal disease. While doing dreamwork I never had a client whose life was so directly threatened but I did have recovering alcoholics dream of relapse. I did field research on dreams and addictions and wrote a white paper titled "The Analysis of a Relapse Dream" that was well received. I was happy to merge my two disciplines as a way of continuing to intervene on such a common and fatal disease.

As my professional and personal interests drew me more and more into dreams and their meaning I began to focus on using the incredible tools I learned at the Jung Institute to make a difference on a broader scale. I wanted to leave a professional legacy that is helpful and available to everyone about a method I found most useful as a deep agent of change. *The Dream Belongs to the Dreamer* is that legacy.

In writing this book, I hope to initiate a renaissance within the mainstream population in both appreciating the power of dreams through dreamwork and the user-friendly subjective symbol immersion method to understanding them. I have a vision of children sharing their dreams and nightmares with their parents around the breakfast table and learning more about who they are and where they fit both in the family and the larger collective. I want lovers to learn more about each other through their dreams thus making a deeper commitment or not. I envision dreamwork as a wondrous healing tool for all. A tool that will enhance understanding between people and reduce conflicts on all levels.

This book will also help you be an effective dream interpreter using the Subjective Symbol Immersion Method (SSIM). SSIM involves all the core concepts of classical analytical theory, from Carl Jung and Sigmund Freud with a sprinkling of Gestalt, Self-Psychology, and Body Centered Therapy as well. All theories and concepts in the book are described in mainstream language and there is a glossary of terms in the back.

You will learn how to take possession of your dream in a rich and rewarding way. You can, in brief focused practice sessions, enhance your self-awareness and enrich your understanding of your inner world. In many cases the Subjective Symbol Immersion Method can provide a sound and meaningful tool to promote deep healing. This hands-on method can be very rewarding in a brief period of time.

This book will also teach you basic dreamwork tools, such as dream theories, how to remember your dreams, and core dream definitions. In addition you will learn and understand why the same dream symbol means different things to different people. If you are a practicing therapist, SSIM will help you help others.

The idea of *taking ownership of your dream* is the heart of the Subjective Symbol Immersion Method. The dream belonging to the dreamer is the core principle that will guide you through the learning experience. Included in the book are practice materials that will aid you in finding the method within this principle.

CHAPTER 1

Understanding the Challenge

The first challenge to my traditional style of working with dreams led to the creation of the Subjective Symbol Immersion Method. It was a defining moment for me, one I thought about for months before my theory evolved. Here's what happened.

One day a client, a young female flight attendant, said these wake-up words to me:

"I don't think that's what it means, Velva."

What? I thought. *Of course that's what it means. I know what I'm doing.* I continued to question her challenge, yet was committed to hearing her out.

"Really? Well, OK, I'm open. Help me out here."

"I think it means I need to find a new job. One that lets me stay home with my kids."

Now, I don't remember the dream but I do remember realizing she was right. In her world that's exactly what the dream meant. I was thinking too much by the book, being too objective and theoretically focused. Too narrow and clearly working outside my client's frame of reference. I wasn't honoring her world, I was honoring the world of clinical theory and practice. After that session I remember thinking, *"Well, it's her dream."* From that day forward I began to look at dreams differently. It wasn't easy.

At first, most of my clients didn't want to do the work. They didn't want to put the time and effort into something they felt so confused about. Something too mysterious. They would say to me words such as, "You're the expert," and, "You know better than I do." I realized I had an entrenched therapeutic model I had foolishly set in stone. Now that's not so bad as clients, like all of us, need predictability. However when it came to dream symbols I realized it was important for all my clients to put their own personal interpretations on the table first. I felt that this approach was like giving them seeds and a shovel, not a free meal. I believed that once they mastered this therapeutic task they would feel more confident and do the necessary digging into their own unconscious to find their own answers to the dream puzzle.

Another change I made was to call myself a Dream Facilitator, not a Dream Analyst. That was helpful for new clients who didn't have any previous experience working with dreams. I also talked about the new, more personal and subjective model to my current clients. Looking back I realized about half of them were able to switch over. Most who did were in the two advanced therapy groups and were able to process the change as a group, thus getting support and encouragement from each other.

Eventually I began to teach this model to my fellow clinicians. It was then I needed to give it the overarching principle of self-discovery. This principle, so vital to personal growth that it fuels the fire of the True Self, is the goal (gold) of all successful depth-psychotherapy. I also felt it was time to find a descriptive and safe container to put this treasure in.

Jungians use the Greek word *temenos* to describe the sacred space of the therapeutic relationship. A relationship bound by integrity, honesty, and trust. The word can also be used to describe a safe container either real such as an urn of ashes or psychological represented by a core value with principles and boundaries. It was time to find a *temenos* for my method but first it needed a descriptive name.

I'd like to say that I got the name from a dream but no such luck. I struggled along, like all people do with new ideas and inspirations. I rejected many names. Not only did it have to include the theory without explanation and lots of words, but it had to sound right too. I remember the first word I picked was the word *subjective.* Subjective means personal. The word *personal* seemed overused and could have sexual vibes so I didn't want that word to color my process, but the word *subjective* worked and it could cross over into both lay and clinical populations. It was also the opposite of *objective,* which meant cold and impersonal. I liked it.

Next I thought about the dream and how to make the dream process manageable. What is it about a dream that clients can get their hands on? Now some dreams can be very long and detailed, with lots of shifts. I had to keep it simple or the process, the training, and the therapeutic hour would turn into endless days. What to do?

Suddenly I thought of the word *symbol,* a word meaning something that represents something else, like the American flag represents patriotism. I knew that all dreams are symbolic and have at least one important symbol. So, Subjective Symbol something. That sounded right. But what about the symbols? What was I doing with them? More importantly for the process, what should be done with them? How could I make understanding symbols the primary goal yet include my pet theorists as well, especially Carl Jung?

That took a lot of thought. Eventually I selected the word *immersion* since that was basically what I was doing. Taking the client's subjective dream symbol and immersing it into an exploratory set of theories, especially Jung's. The next word was easy. It was a method so I chose the word *method.* Thus Subjective Symbol Immersion Method (SSIM) was born.

Next, I needed a guiding principle. One that drove home the subjective aspect of the dream and described the safe container it was in. One that was clear and not open to misinterpretation or challenge. Here I got lucky and didn't have to struggle so long.

The phrase, *the dream belongs to the dreamer,* was born over a dinner table in a popular restaurant called the Basil Leaf Cafe in the Lincoln Park neighborhood of Chicago during a discussion with my friend and colleague Dr. Steve Batten. I recall Steve saying something like, "Right, it's their dream," and my responding, "Yes, the dream belongs to them, not me." Bam! There it was, "The Dream Belongs to the Dreamer." Another defining moment.

I also realized there were two other guiding principles within the Subjective Symbol Immersion Method that needed to be recognized and honored. They too evolved over time and I began to incorporate them as applications to the process along with the dream belongs to the dreamer. They are:

1. Don't literalize the dream. Dreams are symbolic, not literal.
2. Don't moralize a dream. Dreams are neither good nor bad, they just are.

I suggest you write down these three principles or reference points while learning this method. You'll see how much easier dreamwork becomes once you do.

So, what exactly does all this mean to you? How can you implement these guiding principles in the dreamwork process without a professional? I will show you how and throughout the learning experience, if you stick to the guidelines, you too will gain the confidence needed to trust yourself to understand the messages from your inner world. It's time for you to now take possession of your dreams.

CHAPTER II

The Three Guiding Principles

The first principle, *the dream belongs to the dreamer*, means that it is *your* dream and yours alone. You must treasure it completely and guard it as fiercely as you would a vital body part. It is, after all, a segment of your True Self. Practicing this principle will help you go deeper into your unconscious for answers, rather than give yourself away to a symbol book or another outside source. If you can do that, if you can honor your dream and take possession of its symbols, you will be rewarded in ways you cannot yet imagine. Trust the process, take that leap of faith, and watch how the real dream sessions in this book will demonstrate that truth.

Symbol books, although somewhat helpful on an archetypal or stereotypical level, can never, and I mean *never*, tell you what *your* dream and its symbols truly mean to you on a personal, subjective level. A level that allows you to understand who you are and implement the changes needed for personal growth.

At a conference on trust, noted researcher Eugene Gendlin, Ph.D., encouraged attendees to see in his words, "Psyche as a house where dreams come as guests through the unconscious. Welcome them as you would an invited guest. And trust the process."

Unfortunately, the mainstream therapeutic process, determined years ago by the emerging psychoanalytic (Freudian) field, became established as a doctor/patient model. To this day it remains a doctor-patient relationship in many therapeutic practices. Practices where the analyst/doctors are in the know and patients are expected to rely on them, not themselves, for answers. With the advent of higher education, self-help, and psychological research available to all, that's not a realistic therapeutic model in today's world.

In the early years of psychoanalysis, a patient lay silently on the couch while the expert, out of sight, encouraged the patient to meander through his or her unconscious. Today, most patients don't lie on couches, but the belief that analysts have all the answers to dreams and patients don't is still there to a surprising degree. The truth is, the patient is the only one that *really does have the answers* and it is up to the analyst/therapist/counselor to ask the right questions. Questions that help the patient decode his or her thought processes, especially when it comes to dream symbols. Those questions will be scattered throughout the book and outlined for you in a step-by-step section in the *Dreamer's Toolkit.*

To compound the problem, that old belief led to books by dream "experts" who convinced themselves they knew what every symbol meant and dictated definitions. This practice led to more depersonalization of the dream symbol and a disconnect for the person seeking their personal truth and a deeper meaning through dreamwork. If we follow Gendlin's advice and ask ourselves, "What is the gift the dream is bringing me?" a new, deeper response will occur. It's a serious question and one that cannot be answered by a symbol book. It can however be answered by using the Subjective Symbol Immersion Method (SSIM) created for just this purpose.

Another way to look at personalizing your dreams is to imagine the dream as your best friend (it is). After all, it comes from your deepest truth and don't we look to our best friends to tell us the truth, the whole truth, even if it's something we don't want to hear? Just imagine on the most profound level what it would be like for you to learn the truth about that job you didn't get or the person who left you without honestly telling you why. All the consolations of your family and friends couldn't make a dent in that reality. You would finally know your vulnerabilities and have a way to strengthen them. You'd be free to go about the necessary changes, or not. Changes that would help you be more authentic, more self-accepting, more who you were meant to be. What a relief that would be! It's a relief just knowing it's doable and that *you can do it.* Wouldn't you like to know how? That's what this is all about. It's a way to tell you how in an easy, user-friendly way. You'll find the first lesson in understanding the importance of the primary symbol in Julia's upsetting repetitive dream.

Don't literalize the dream, means everything and everyone in the dream is symbolic. This is particularly important if you have a sexual dream and are afraid to share it or experience shame about it. One client dreamed of having sex with his sister and after doing SSIM he realized it didn't mean that at all as a matter of fact, it wasn't really his sister in the dream but a dream figure that resembled her. Other dreamers learn they are taking on the dark sexual energy of someone they are close to and experience the dream as a warning dream.

If you are riding in a car, you are not. You are taking a journey and the car represents that journey. You can't fly, you aren't a bird nor a fish swimming under water yet many people have those dreams. The person you loved and lost didn't come back from the grave yet many dream of them. A childhood friend can represent lost innocence, not the actual child who is now an adult. These flying, swimming, lost love or child dreams are meant as messages to the dreamer to look at something about those things, not the things themselves. So, guiding principle number two is *don't literalize the dream.*

Finally, don't moralize about a dream. Everything is symbolic therefore neither good nor bad. Symbols and Shadows are simply present in your dream as messengers. This is important if you have a sexual dream and take it literally, leading you to judge yourself and others because of it. Don't! Doing so will impede your progress and may even keep you from learning a vital truth. In addition, when you finally recognize your Shadow, that great source of suppressed energy and creativity, you will need to embrace, transform, and integrate it to be whole. That will be very hard to do if you judge it.

In the next chapter you will meet Julia and join us in her dream session. Pay attention to the process and see what tools were used by both Julia and me to help her discover her transformative truth.

CHAPTER III

Finding the Primary Symbol—Julia's Dream

I often tell my clients that repetitive dreams-dreams that present the same symbol over and over again-are like a nagging mother, a mother that keeps at you to wear your warm hat or boots until you do, just to stop her nagging. Once you personally interpret the dream symbol from a repetitive dream it will never come back, just like your mother stopped nagging when you finally put your hat and boots on.

The following dream is a good example of what I mean about nagging dreams and what can be learned from them. In this repetitive dream we're using the Gestalt approach; that is a method where the dreamer imagines *becoming* the symbol in the dream. It is a method you'll learn more about in following chapters. Here's what happened.

A colleague called me one day with a referral. She had a client who was having an upsetting repetitive dream and asked if I would see her. I agreed and a week later a middle-aged woman, let's call her Julia, appeared at my door twisting a hankie in her hands. She looked terrible. Dull grayish hair, bags under her eyes, and defeated body language told me she was in trouble. I imagined her repetitive dream to be a nightmare, one that woke her up screaming. I took her arm and led her to the couch. She sat down and wept. She told me that she didn't sleep and didn't even want to go to bed anymore, then added how grateful she was to see me as she was at the end of her "emotional rope."

"I'm glad you're here, Julia. Anne (her therapist) told me how upset you are and how much trouble you have sleeping."

"It's been a nightmare for me. My life is on hold. I just can't believe this is happening to me." She muffled a sob.

I took her free hand. "Tell me the dream."

She looked up, eyes filled with both exhaustion and tears, and said, "I dream of a ringing phone. The phone keeps on ringing and ringing and ringing and no one answers it."

I could barely contain my surprise. "That's it?"

"Yes," she replied, "that's the whole dream. It never changes."

After my initial reaction I was relieved to know that the ringing phone was the primary symbol, as that part of the process can take time. "OK. Let's get to work. How old are you in the dream?" (That is important to know as it sets the time frame for the buried issue and trauma.)

"My age. The age I am now."

"Where are you in the dream?"

Julia paused a minute, then replied, "I think it's my house but I'm not one hundred per cent sure."

"Is anyone else in the dream?"

"No, and I don't see myself in the dream either. I don't see anyone or anything but that ringing phone. It's madness."

"OK. That's good. That's very helpful. Where is the ringing phone?"

"I don't know. The phone is sort of floating in space, just ringing and ringing."

I told her that the primary (and only) symbol was the phone and we would be working exclusively on how to understand what that symbol meant to her. I explained to her that it is not really a ringing phone but a symbol of something else, obviously something very important since the dream is repetitive, and bubbling up from her unconscious demanding attention. I checked the time. Forty minutes to go.

"Julia, describe the phone to me."

"It's funny you should ask since the dream is always about a floating phone that doesn't stop ringing, but the phone changes. Sometimes it's an old rotary phone, sometimes it's a push button, other times it has a cord, and sometimes it doesn't have a cord. Is that important?"

"Yes, that's very helpful. Now tell me if any of those phones are familiar to you. Do you recognize any of them?" (The more details the dreamer can recall, the quicker the connections she can make between her past and current realities.)

"Not really, I thought about that."

"OK. Good. Now, what colors are they?"

"Usually white, but now that I think about it, it was a funny sort of glowing white, not a real color. One phone was the kind that hangs on a wall, like a kitchen phone. Another was a desktop model." She looked at me and managed a wan smile, then asked, "Remember the Princess phone? Well, one of them was that style. I remember having one of those in our bedroom." She suddenly looked more alert.

"Good. That's good work, Julia."

"Now that we're talking about them, I'm beginning to realize those models were all over the house. I had phones in the hall, the kitchen, my bedroom, even the laundry room." We both smiled at the last one.

"Good! Things are starting to percolate. You're connecting some dots." The end table clock told me there were thirty minutes left, and I wanted her to experience the relief she needed by the end of the session. I was hopeful.

One thing a clinician needs to pay attention to in a session is the time. Decisions need to be made early on whether there is time for a deeper probing as it is vital not to leave the client emotionally bleeding at the end of a session. In addition, I was working with another therapist's client and didn't want to have her return for a second session unless absolutely necessary.

Suddenly things ground to a halt. Nothing I asked Julia went anywhere. Time was flying. I decided to apply the Gestalt method to her dreamwork, the method where the dreamer imagines becoming the symbol. I said, "OK, Julia, we're running out of time. I want you to *be* the phone."

"Excuse me?"

"It's a dreamwork method I use called Gestalt. It works well by asking the dreamer to be the symbol in the dream. I want you to *be* the phone. Imagine you are that glimmering white phone just ringing and ringing and ringing. Let's use the Princess phone image to help you focus. I am going to relax you and together we will bring you into that space. That space where *you* are the ringing Princess phone. OK?"

She looked at me with alarm. "Will I be hypnotized?"

"No, not at all, don't worry, just be very relaxed. Relaxation helps your imagination kick in so you can be that ringing Princess phone. I will lead you through a series of deep breathing exercises to help you relax. When you become that ringing phone ask yourself, 'Why doesn't anyone answer me?'"

Julia set aside her twisted handkerchief, put both feet on the floor, closed her eyes, and began the deep breathing exercises. Five minutes later I could see through her body language, that she was deeply relaxed.

I said softly, "Now Julia *you* are the glimmering white Princess phone just ringing and ringing. Imagine what that feels like. Experience the vibrations. Immerse yourself into them. Imagine what it is like to sit on a bedside table ringing and ringing and ringing. Feel the tabletop supporting you. Can you imagine those things?" She nodded.

"Good Julia, now see your receiver (remember she *is* the phone) sitting on top of you, like an arm draped over your shoulder. Ask yourself why no one is picking your arm up. Why no one is stopping you from ringing. Why no one is answering you. Keep asking those questions of yourself until you get an answer that works for you. Take your time and continue your deep breathing. The answers are there, inside of you, inside of that white ringing phone you have become."

I checked the time again, hoping the remaining ten minutes would be enough. I decided if it wasn't I would comp Julia an extra ten minutes as a courtesy to my colleague. If that still wasn't enough time, I feared I was out of options as the Gestalt method is the last trick in my dream bag. I found myself watching her and called upon my inner cheerleader to send some relief her way. Suddenly she stirred. I straightened up.

Just as I was about to ask her what was going on Julia sprang to life and, smiling broadly, said, "I've got it!"

Relief. "Tell me."

"I really *am* the phone. All the phones. I've been the family switchboard for as long as I can remember (hence the changing models). If my husband wanted to tell my son something he told me to tell him. If my daughter wanted to tell her brother or father something she asked me to tell them for her. And I did. I did it for years and years. Aunts, uncles, in-law, them too."

"Good work, Julia!" I exclaimed, then paused. "It's a powerful role. You were the lynchpin in the family communication system. Pretty heady stuff."

She agreed it made her feel important and not left out, especially when the kids got older. I asked her to look at why no one picked up the phone in the dream. At first she feared it was because her family didn't want to talk to her anymore, but then, after deeper thought, Julia realized no one was picking up the phone because she didn't want that role anymore. The role was exhausting her. She told me she was in therapy to change and now saw that part of that change was not being the family switchboard anymore. She told me it was a great relief even thinking about letting go of that burden. We also agreed it was a deceptively toxic role for all involved and in the way of her getting a life for herself.

Julia left the session happy and so was I. A week later my colleague called and told me Julia was sleeping soundly, the dream hadn't returned, and family sessions were in the works.

The interesting thing about this particular dream session was that Julia had never had a full-fledged dream about the phone, just one dream fragment with one symbol, the ringing phone, nagging her to take action. It's a good example of how a dream fragment can be a powerful agent of change. In addition she and I never even discussed the various theoretical models, types of dreams, or archetypes. Those ideas and techniques that are often necessary in dreamwork.

In the next chapter you'll meet the theorists, their theories and begin to learn how you can apply them to your particular dream if need be.

CHAPTER IV

Our Theoretical Guides—A Brief Introduction

The Subjective Symbol Immersion Method's (SSIM) theoretical foundation is a combination of psychological theorists and theories. Carl Jung, Sigmund Freud, Gestalt, and Eugene Gendlin. First and foremost is my personal hero and clinical guide, C. G. Jung.

Carl Gustav Jung, 1875-1961. Jung was a Swiss psychiatrist who, after splitting with Freud, founded the school of analytical psychology. He believed that neuroses (fear and anxiety) represented a mind out of balance and that understanding one's dreams was a way to regain that balance. Jung defined dreams as "Independent, spontaneous manifestations of the unconscious; fragments of involuntary psychic activity just conscious enough to be reproducible in a waking state." In other words, we have no conscious awareness of the stuff that makes up a dream until we sleep and lose conscious control of our thoughts then hopefully retrieve them upon awakening. He goes on to say, "Dreams are natural phenomena which are nothing other than what they present to be. They do not deceive, they do not lie, they do not distort or disguise; *they are invariably seeking to express something that the ego does not know and does not understand.*"

Jung also believed dreams picture the current situation in the psyche from the point of view of the unconscious, which works mainly on a symbolic level. Whereas Freud viewed dreams as wish fulfillment with procreation (sexual energy) as the driving force, Jung believed dreams reveal aspects of oneself that transcend sexuality. Moreover he felt dreams reveal unconscious motivations and present new points of view across the whole of the human condition, especially in conflicting situations. Jung used story to help explain his views. He states: "*The whole dreamwork is essentially subjective, and a dream is a theater in which the dreamer is himself the scene, the player, the prompter, the producer, the author, the public and the critic.*"

Sigmund Freud: 1856-1939. Freud was an Austrian physician and the founder of psychoanalysis. Among tenets of Freudian theory are that human beings are motivated by a pleasure principle and dreams are based on his theory that everything is driven by pleasure. Freud also recognized conscious and unconscious levels of mental activity. He taught that all symbols were sexual in nature, thus leaving no room for the dreamer to explore his or her own connections. Adopting Freud's theories into SSIM on occasion makes sense since the dreamer may in fact gain some insight into a complex dream symbol from Freud's perspective *as long as the dream and the symbol remain in the dreamer's possession.*

Gestalt Method. The Gestalt method is defined as a physical, biological, psychological, or symbolic pattern of elements so unified as a whole that its parts cannot be discovered from an examination or understanding of it entirety. In other words, the whole is bigger than the sum of the parts. For example, once a chef has blended all the spices and other ingredients into a delicious stew then simmers it into a sensational dish, neither he nor anyone else can undo the magic or explain how it tastes by simply listing the ingredients. Another example is imagining that you are a shoe and experiencing all the things a shoe experiences. Being laced up, having high heels, walking on grass or concrete, being too cramped, going through puddles of rainwater, etc.

If you recall Julia's dream in the previous chapter you'll further understand how the Gestalt method works by remembering I asked her to *be* the white ringing princess phone and what insight she gained when that happened.

Eugene Gendlin: 1926-present. Gendlin developed a way of measuring the extent to which a client can recognize a felt sense that affirms who they truly are. He named his technique *focusing.* Focusing is an introspective *psychological tool* in which the dreamer focuses on subtle physical sensations that underlie his or her greater emotional experiences. This method helps the dreamer gain an understanding of his or her problems from these smaller sensations and encourages them to continue seeking answers. The method is very helpful when there are body shifts and other physical clues apparent when working on a dream symbol. Going back to Julia's dream, knowing this method helped me understand (when she began to stir during her dream symbol work) that she had gained a deeper awareness of the ringing white phone. *Also note this technique was used during the Gestalt process so it is possible to combine two or more theories in the same dream session.*

CHAPTER V

To the Heart of Your Dreams

You may be part of a dream group, or working with a dream partner, or listening to your child's dreams over breakfast. Whatever the situation, always bear in mind to abide by the principle that the dream is the possession of the dreamer. Within this principle is the Greek term Jung used called *temenos.* The word means a sacred space or a safe place to share your inner world. For therapists it's symbolic container that means keeping boundaries when working with others.

If you're working with others, the questions you need to ask in order to be most helpful to them, while honoring this rule, are in this book. You may even discover new and more meaningful questions over time that will be even more helpful. The important thing is to not lose your boundaries and don't violate a trust. Let the dreamer keep the dream just as Julia was able to with her dream of the ringing telephone. Remember how she benefited from embracing that principle?

The following process will give you a map to the treasures that lie within your dream symbols. Just like finding real treasures it's easiest to begin with a map to get started. It helps to think of it this way because, in a very real sense, this whole book is a treasure map that helps you discover not just any treasure, but your own unique gold mine. The gold nuggets that trickle up in the twilight of your sleep are for you to discover and make sense of. It will be a different reward for each reader. That's why SSIM was created and what makes it so remarkably effective.

These gold nuggets are in the form of symbols and sometimes there are so many symbols that the wisest thing to do is discover the primary one, the one that has the most energy for you, then examine and understand it. That then becomes a touchstone for your learning experience.

Let's start by keeping things manageable. SSIM will be expanded and explained throughout this book using other actual dreams to demonstrate its effectiveness. Meanwhile let's begin with an exercise using three primary Signposts. Imagine a map with only a few locations on it. A map where you'll have to go from place to place, like Jason and his quest for the Golden Fleece, or your own Hero's Journey where the challenges are great and the rewards life affirming. Later you'll be filling in the roads and byways that lead you deeper into your True Self. What a priceless discovery!

To get started on this important first step write down a simple dream in the spaces below. For now it's best to keep it short and doable.

____

____

Next, look at the illustration below and fill in the responses in the box to the left of the Signposts. Remember, the primary symbol is *the thing or person that has the most energy for you.* The thing or person in the dream you *emotionally respond to the most.* The one object or person that keeps coming back to you as you think about the dream. It can be anything, anything at all but it *can be only one.* Remember too that if it is a person, the person is symbolic, not literal. In other words, if it's your boss, he or she probably represents authority. Take your time, *it's very important to find the primary symbol first.*

Once you accomplish this, the next piece of the puzzle is to stay *completely focused on the primary symbol* and really think about what it means to you. Ask yourself why it is appearing in your dream and why now? Why is the primary symbol so emotionally charged? What type of emotions do you feel when you think of it. Fear? Passion? Grief? *The important thing is to stay focused on it and on nothing else in the dream until you get that part understood.* If you're struggling please trust that your treasure will eventually be revealed. The more you dig the clearer the answers will become. If you need to, do the *Radiating Exercise.* This means taking a plain piece of paper and drawing the primary symbol in a circle in the middle and then draw lines radiating out of it every time you have a thought or idea of why you react the way you do to the primary symbol. Eventually you will have a "Gendlin Aha!" moment like Julia did about her white Princess phone symbol.

If you are still having trouble identifying the primary symbol, that's OK, you'll get there. Just go back over the dream and circle all the objects and people in the dream and then make a list. Go down the list allowing yourself time to feel and experience the words you've written down. Here's where your gut comes in. Close your eyes and let your felt-sense about the object or person on your list percolate in your mind. Be patient. Give yourself time.

If you are still struggling, do the opposite exercise, that is, eliminate the objects and people that leave you feeling really flat.

Still stuck? Take a break. Do something else for a while. Something Zen-like such as washing dishes or raking leaves. Give your psyche a rest. When you feel refreshed go back over your list and settle on three choices as the possible primary symbol. Go over each one, pausing as you think about them. Close your eyes, letting your feelings bubble to the surface. You *can* trust your gut, that's its purpose, to act as a signaling device. Your signaling device. Whatever you do, *don't give up!*

Think of the third Signpost as the third step that will create a major connection between the present and the past. Ask yourself when was the first time you remember having the feeling that the primary dream symbol triggered. How old were you? Where were you? Do you remember who was with you and what you were wearing? Did you have something in your hand or a toy or pet at you feet? It's at this point every little detail becomes a dot and before you know it, all the dots connect to the road not yet traveled and your journey to your True Self.

It's extremely important to complete this exercise as it is the foundation of your journey home, and like a car, you want a strong carriage carrying you forward. The trip will be much faster and easier when you've accomplished this step.

Finally, once you have mastered the primary symbol and discovered what it means to you and why, this book will help you go back over the dream in a more detailed manner. It will help you explore the various byways that flesh out your map and lead to even deeper places in your psyche (mind). Think of those next smaller steps as following a trail of small golden nuggets that lead to the main vein. Don't get discouraged, the payoff as you saw in Julia's dream will be tremendous.

Here's the illustrated outline of Signposts to help you get organized and begin to practice the process. Write the primary symbol you identified from the dream you to the left of the Signpost #1.

In Signpost #2 write down what the symbol means to you in the space on the left. If you need more room just grab a piece of paper and follow along with the Signposts. Feel free to refer back to any of the material presented so far.

To complete Signpost #3 connect the symbol and your understanding of it from the first two Signposts to a past or present experience or situation. This may take time. It's important that you don't skip this Signpost because it gives the dream and its primary symbol its deepest meaning. Please do not go forward in the book until you've completed this exercise as the next steps in the process are dependent on it.

First Major Stop: Signpost #1.

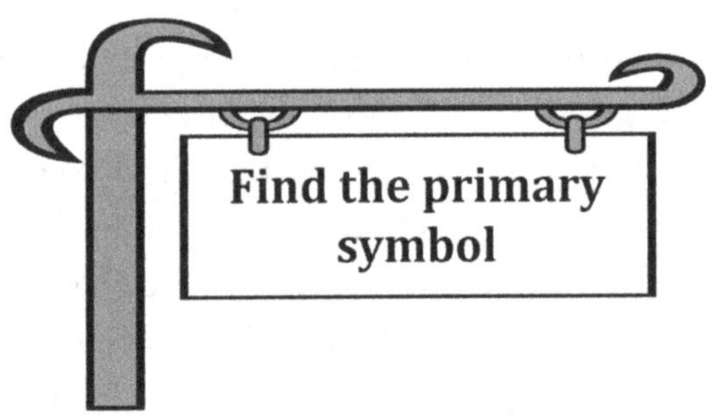

Second Major Stop: Signpost #2.

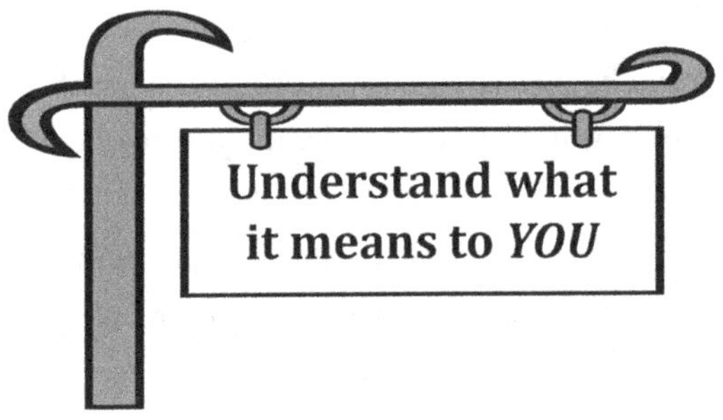

Third Major Stop: Signpost #3.

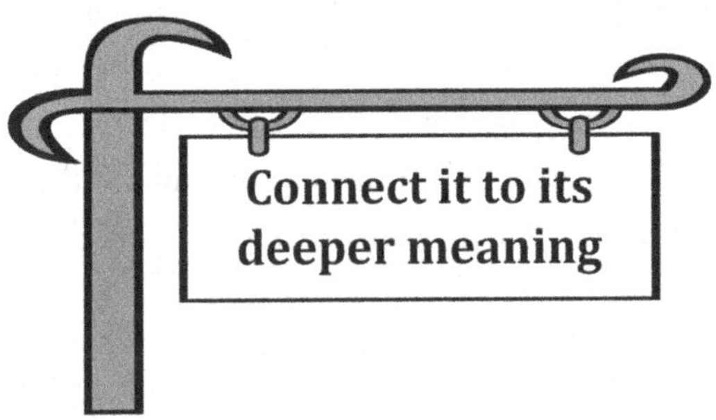

Now that you have completed the three primary Signposts get a clean piece of paper and rewrite the dream you've been working on. Go over it and circle or underline the parts of the dream that you can group under the three Signposts. Remember, not everything will fit neatly into these categories but recognize the ones that do. Keep at it. These are merely Signposts. The other undiscovered parts of the dream are the golden nuggets that lead you to the deepest vein.

It's very, very important here to understand that dreams and dream symbols have many depths. Often when dreamers complete this exercise they do gain insight, feel accomplished, and have a tendency to stop. *Don't.* The vein you mined will peter out and quitting now will cheat you out of the main treasure, the golden mother lode of your True Self.

If you can hang in there and push through to a deeper level you'll be able to answer the step-by-step questions about the dream that need your insight. It will be challenging and as you drill down expect many feelings to surface. That is a good thing. Perhaps you can start a feeling journal or leave a wide margin on your dreamwork page to jot them down. Understand that on a very basic level we all are our feelings first and foremost. Many of us bury our feelings, especially the painful ones, and that's part of the challenge of deep healing. We must feel them, embrace them, and transform the dark ones (what Jung calls the Shadow) into the light. Only then will you be free of them once and for all. It will be such a blessed relief when that happens you'll feel reborn. What a gift.

Before you move on to the next part of the exercise I'd like to help you create your own *temenos* or sacred space for the deeper healing. Some of you may have a sanctuary already. Many do. Perhaps it's a special place in your home or a nearby park or garden. Wherever it is once you begin your deeper healing it's a good idea to go there if continuing this process becomes fearful. For those of you who don't have a sacred space or *temenos* here's what to do.

First, gather four primary stones no larger than a baby's fist or golf ball. You can mark these stones North, South, East and West after determining the directions from your location. Next place the four primary stones facing their marked directions making sure they are far enough apart for you to sit and write in. Once your directions are determined fill in the rest of the circle with smaller stones, once again making sure you can comfortably fit inside the circle. You can also place the stones around your desk or writing area at home if that works for you.

Understand that your *temenos* needn't be a permanent sacred space as the stones can be removed and placed in other areas as you see fit. *The idea is that the space within the circle of stones is sacred* no matter where you build your *temenos.* Step inside and sit down. If it doesn't feel right, do it again in another location until your felt-sense tells you your sacred space is in the right spot. Some of my clients who travel for a living carry their *temenos* stones in a pouch or box so they are right on hand. Other clients have purchased white sage and used it in a cleansing ritual after their circle was complete. Whatever works.

You are now ready to excavate and explore your dream on a deeper level. Congratulations! You're on your way.

CHAPTER VI

The Primary Symbol

The heart of the Subjective Symbol Immersion Method or SSIM is finding and identifying the primary symbol. By now you should have done that. If not, stop and go back to the previous chapter and continue working on the three signposts. Don't be discouraged. *You can do it.* If you have to, guess. Guesses are often very intuitive.

Now that you have your dream and its primary symbol, get your pen/pencil and paper, go to your sacred space, and write the dream down again, this time looking for the story of the dream. For example, let's go back to Julia's dream. Julia would have written, "I dreamed there was a ringing phone that no one answered. It kept ringing and ringing and ringing." If Julia were following this book she would then answer the following five questions.

a. Who is in the dream? (cast of characters)
b. What is happening in the dream? (action)

c. Where does the dream take place? (setting)
d. When or what is the time frame of the dream? (past or present)
e. Why did the dream appear now?

The *Who* is Julia. The *When* is both the past and the present (different era phones); the *What*, or action, is limited to the ringing phone. The *Where* in Julia's dream is a somewhat vague house. I think it is vague for a reason. I believe her unconscious wanted Julia to pay strict attention to just the Princess phone and its powerful message. Now, if you recall, it was the *Why?* that generated the most work on Julia's part. Julia needed to dig deep, it was her dream. In this case, Julia used the Gestalt method of *being* the symbol to experience and understand the full meaning of her dream and how exhausting her role had become.

It's very helpful to know the story or theme of a dream right away, especially if it is a long or complicated dream. In Julia's case it was simply a story of a ringing phone that no one answered. Short story indeed, but a story nevertheless. If you recall her reply to the second question, "*Where* are you in the dream?" was "a house." The next question was, "How old are you in the dream?" was that, "I was my current age." So we have the setting, a house, Julia as the main character, the action, a ringing phone, and a time-frame. Try to visualize it. This will help you in visualizing the story in your dream.

Now it's time for you to understand the story of your dream. The following set of four questions will help you. You can also go back to the previous set of five questions if you wish. *Remember, by now you need to know what the primary symbol is.* If you don't, go back and find it.

What is the theme of my dream?

The theme of the dream can be unearthed by the action in or story of the dream. Are you looking for something (a Quest Dream) or going somewhere (a Journey Dream)? If you're feeling stuck, think about a film, play, or movie to help you typecast it. Still stuck? Look in Reference II in the back for a description of other types of dreams.
Answer: ______________________________

Where am I in my dream?

It's common to not know where you are in a dream. Often people say a house or a car or "I don't know." If you don't know where you are, guess. If it's a vague, floating kind of place, write that down. The more nuggets you fill in the clearer the dream will become to you and soon you'll have a much better idea of where you are. It's fine. Trust the process.
Answer: ______________________________

How old am I in my dream?

Knowing your age in a dream is helpful because the experience or memory the dream wants you to remember, focus on, and possibly heal from, occurred during that age. The younger you are in the dream the more challenging it will be so here's the rewarding Inner Child Exercise to help tap into your memory bank.
Answer: ______________________________

Inner Child Exercise

Sit down, close your eyes, and see your young self. If you're having trouble doing that dig up some old family or school pictures. When you see yourself in the dream what is the look on your face? Sad? Smiling? Write that down. Next check out your haircut, clothes and shoes. What are you wearing? Get very detailed here, i.e. socks? Also, remembering Gendlin's felt-sense with all its nuances, such as posture or position. Do you have downcast eyes? Are you sitting, standing, or slumping? Perhaps you are holding something or there is a toy or pet at your feet. *The more details the better.* For reference, write the answers here.

____

____

____

____

____

____.

Who else is in your dream?

> Finally, write down all the people in the dream and their ages. If no one is in the dream with you then write down "Me." If people are in the dream and they leave write that down as that becomes part of the action. If it starts with "Me" and people enter later write them down as they will become part of the action too. It's important. If in fact you are alone in

the dream or witnessing the dream such as Julia write that down too.

Answer: ______________________________

____

____

____

____

______________________________.

It's perfectly normal for these steps to stir up feelings of anxiety, fear, and/or sadness for some dreamers. Sometimes all three. It's OK to stop here for a while and go to your sacred space and journal what you are experiencing. *Both activities will help you integrate your dream material into your consciousness and that is exactly what this process is all about. The more conscious you are, the more whole you become. The more whole you become, the more centered and confident you'll be.* A great reward! Also, don't be afraid of any shadow material (dark feelings). We all have shadow issues and they need to be integrated too. Once you acknowledge them by bringing them into the light you'll discover they have a way of mysteriously disappearing, leaving behind a wake of newly found freedom and energy at your disposal. In addition, you'll feel stronger and more secure. Isn't that great!

Good job! Now is a good time to regroup and integrate the work you have done so far. I strongly encourage you to journal and process all that you are learning and the feelings that have come up. We'll be digging down to the mother lode in the next chapter and it will be wonderful for you to feel more centered and confident when we do. There will be additional challenges that I'm sure you can rise to if you've come this far, done the necessary work, and journaled about it. Not sure? Here's a checklist for you to look over before we move on.

- Do I know how to find the primary symbol in a dream?
- Do I know the story of my dream?
- Do I know the theme of my dream?
- Have I created a sacred space or temenos to do my dreamwork in?
- Do I have a Feelings Journal?
- Do I have a Dream Journal?
- Am I ready to go deeper?

Finally, don't forget to pay special attention to your dreams right now.

CHAPTER VII

Deeper Work with Symbols

Remember that the primary symbol is all about what it means to you. It's yours and yours alone. Here are other questions to help you uncover deeper meanings and begin to connect more dots. Questions that are like little nuggets of gold that lead to the rich vein of your True Self. As you further relate to the main symbol ask yourself these additional questions.

What does the primary symbol represent to you?
Answer: ______________________________

What memories are emerging?
Answer: ______________________________

What feelings are emerging?
Answer: ______________________________

How do the memories and feelings connect?

Answer: ___________________________

If you have worked through these questions you should have a sense of confidence and mastery about your dream by now. You may think, "Hey, that was easy" and be ready to move on. *Don't.* Instead, continue digging for the deeper rewards in your dream and follow the outline in this chapter. On the other hand, this is your dreamwork so if you wish to move on to another more complex dream go ahead, just go back to the three Signposts to begin exploring it.

The following step-by-step guide to excavating the full meaning of your dream can best be achieved by going methodically through the outline below. Once again get a pencil/pen and paper and write down your answers. This is meant to be a thorough overview of your life situation, both past and present and will take time. Resist the urge to dash the answers off just to get through it. That's just cheating yourself. *If at any point you experience strong feelings or toxic memories come up, try to see that as a good and necessary thing.* Hang in there and let the hero within you prevail and win. You owe it to yourself. And remember you can always stop and take a break. Some people imagine their Inner Child and send him or her warmth and support as needed. You can do that too, just go back to the exercise in Chapter IV where you pictured your Inner Child in such detail.

Time to get started, just follow the outline and *don't skip ahead.*

Outline

A. Connect the Symbol to Its Deeper Meaning.
   1. Look at your present situation. (Important: Don't jump backwards yet.)
      a. Relationships (this includes with yourself).
      b. Family (of origin and/or immediate).
      c. Job, Career, School (recent changes).
      d. Community (neighborhood, general and specific).
      e. Health (illnesses, recent injuries, etc.).
      f. Spirituality and/or religion.
      g. Finances.

   2. Look at your past situation.
      a. Family (broken or intact).
      b. Family History (Grandparents, for example).
      c. Family Secrets (Suspicions?).
      d. Relationships (this includes with yourself).
      e. Job, Career, School (Were you labeled as a child?).
      f. Community or communities (childhood up to college).
      g. Health (childhood illnesses).
      h. Spirituality (or religious affiliation past or present).
      i. Finances or Economic Status of Family of Origin.

B. Connect Present and Past Situations. Use your felt-sense to help you.

1. Exercise:

Write down the current situations that carry the most energy for you and compare them to categories a. through i. in past situations. Stay open as very different subjects can connect, often more than once. Write them down.

____

____

____

____

____

____.

If your felt-sense is feeling alarmed, if you feel anxious and/or panicky it's OK to stop and rest here. If you feel exhausted it's fine to take a nap. It's understandable if you stop all together for a while. *Just don't give up.* Also, don't defer to others. It's your journey. If you don't remember something, resist the urge to call a relative or friend and ask. The memories and answers are yours, they are within you and your goal is to mine your own gold. *No one can do that for you.* On the other hand it's OK to ask for support. We all need that. Above all, *stay true to your journey.*

If you are ready and able to push on, by all means do so. Here is a good time to apply what you are learning to the Three Primary Selves that will ultimately psychologically unite in what Jung called the Trancendent Function. The Transcendent

Function is the part of your psyche that continuously unites feelings and intellect to create a third and higher experience. An experience that contributes to the ongoing formation of the True Self. It is pure and inexpressible. Think of joy. We can experience it but we can never articulate or fully describe it. The Three Primary Selves are:

The Frightened Self.
The Fearless Self.
The True Self.

When you contemplate these three think of a circle, you can even draw one where the three selves are in constant motion, each triggering and contributing to the others. The goal of course is integrating the Frighten and the Fearless Selves into the True Self. Here is where the idea of the Hero's Journey is born and becomes its own reward. The more the Fearless Self wins the battle the sooner the True Self becomes authentic and can emerge.

To help understand this Jung wrote extensively about the Epigenetic Principle of personal growth. The term was borrowed from botany and meant a plant's ability to fully grow and bloom. In psychology it is meant as the innate desire/push to reach our full potential. To be all we can be. He believed psyche is constantly evolving and the integration process goes on throughout our lifetime. You'll discover, as I did, that the more you overcome your fears, the easier it will be to do so.

When I first started my journey I used the image of the Wicked Witch of the West from *The Wizard of Oz.* The image where she melts simply by throwing water on her. It was very helpful. Eventually I came to realize I had outgrown my fears and just didn't know it. All I needed was water from my Heroic Self. *You too can outgrow most of your fears.* Make a commitment right now to let your Hero's Journey begin with trusting your dreams.

I'd like to add here that I always trust what the dream reveals, however upsetting, since I truly believe that if this material has gotten past my unconscious defense structure, I'm ready to handle it.

As you go through this process, integrate your feelings and as you push through to the deeper levels you'll see what I mean. Think about all your learning curves that were scary. Swimming for example. Try to picture the baby who falls and in spite of being hurt gets up and continues on. It's in our nature to move forward. It's "life's longing for itself," over and over again. In addition, we all go through Erik Erickson's eight developmental stages (see glossary), one stage building on another. If we can do it as babies and toddlers, we can do it as adults. *You can do it.* You can go through the dream developmental stages of the Subjective Symbol Immersion Method (SSIM) with that same life's longing. The need to be more. The need to find your purpose. Things we cannot do without a sense of the True Self. *Don't give up.* Take the gift of the dream your Inner Guide has sent you, then tap into you Heroic Self to find your "more."

In the following chapter you'll read how Bill trusted the process, tapped into his feelings, took possession of his dream and became whole. You'll see once again how the three guiding principles, the dream belongs to the dreamer and not literalizing and moralizing dream material led to remarkable results for Bill.

CHAPTER VIII

The Subjective Nature of Dreams—Bill's Dream

Remember you can never have another's dream nor can someone have yours, even though they may be similar. That is the core truth of SSIM and every aspect of this method is built around that core truth. Once you read Bill's dream you will finally and fully understand the subjective nature of a dream. You will see that no one, absolutely no one, could have Bill's dream and grasp where it went and how it healed him other than himself. In addition, it was the last dream Bill brought to our sessions since it led to the completion of his therapeutic journey not long afterward. His process and resulting insight through this dream was remarkable. No book, no therapist, no dream expert, no one except Bill, the dreamer, could have ever correctly interpreted the following dream;

Bill was a 56-year-old recovering alcoholic. The older of two boys, he was raised in an alcoholic family system. Bill's mother was told she couldn't have children, so after he was born he carried her grateful miracle-baby energy into adulthood. His sib was adopted as an infant when Bill was three. A core part of him still thought he was very special. Bill had been sober nearly twenty years when he told me this dream.

"I dreamed I was attracted to my twelve year old niece and made sexual advances toward her. In the dream she was tall, thin, with bright red hair and golden brown skin. She was wearing a thin, white, filmy dress that covered her from her neck to her feet that I could almost see through. I wanted her terribly. I woke up with an erection."

Bill was very upset by the dream. He canceled his regular Sunday visit to his brother's house and told me he was never going there again until his niece was either away at college or married. We had worked on dreams before so he was comfortable when I suggested we use the Subjective Symbol Immersion Method to reveal the dream's secrets. I reminded him that the dream belonged to him and that it was always a bad idea not only to take a dream literally, but to moralize and judge it too. Here's how the session went.

"Bill, how old are you in the dream?"

"My age now."

"Good. Other than your niece is there anyone else in the dream?

"No, just the two of us."

"OK. Fine. Tell me about your niece. What does she look like?"

"My niece is just a kid, a twelve-year-old kid. She's pudgy, certainly not sexy at all, given the kids today, and doesn't look anything like the girl in the dream."

"How do you know it's her then?"

"I just know. Trust me. I'm sure of it."

"OK. I do. It's your dream. Tell me more about your niece."

"Well, like I said, she's pudgy, kind of nerdy. Brown hair, some acne, shortish."

"Does she flirt with you when you visit?"

"God, no! She's only twelve. I remember when I was twelve. It's an awful age."

"Tell me about when you were twelve."

"I was miserable. My father hated me. You know that. He was jealous of all the attention my mother lavished on me. He never got that I hated it. Felt smothered by it. Did I ever tell you I hid in the basement when he came home drunk?"

"No. I didn't know that. Go on."

"Twelve was when I had my first drink and began smoking."

"Hmmm. Now let's look at the dream again. Where are you in the dream?"

"We're in a house, an old house."

"Is the house familiar?"

"Yes and no. Wait! I remember we were in the basement sort of like the one I grew up in, but not. It was fixed up like a rec room. The real old house didn't have a finished basement, just the laundry room."

"That's good. You're starting to connect the dots." (His present was beginning to connect to his past.) A painful past where coming of age was fraught with fear and confusion. "Good work! Anything else about the basement?"

"Well, it's where I used to go to sneak a drink and smoke."

"More dots. Anything else coming up when you remember that?"

"Yeah. I remember how sick I got. Coughing, nauseous. I

use to throw up in the laundry tub. It was disgusting. I must have been out of my mind."

There was a pause in the session where Bill clearly was going back to that scared kid. He sat quietly, looking down at his hands, deep in thought. I waited for the body shift articulated so well by Gendlin in *Let Your Body Interpret Your Dreams,* to indicate an insight. Suddenly Bill straightened up and looked at me with a quizzical expression. I had to make a decision then. Do I pursue his reflective moment or move forward with the dream? I let his body language lead me. I responded to his quizzical, now-what look. Also, we had worked together long enough for me to know that had he wanted to share a deeper moment at that time, he would have. Finally, the upsetting dream was what the session was all about so I decided to stay on track.

I nodded, indicating I understood. "Now tell me, what is the strongest image or symbol in the dream? What has the most energy for you?"

"My niece. Definitely my niece. Why do you think she looked like that?"

"Like what?"

"You know, tall, thin, golden brown skin. A white filmy dress."

"Bright red hair too," I added.

"Yes, really bright, shimmery."

"Well, Bill, if we don't take the dream literally, if the image of your niece is a symbol, what is it a symbol of? What is thin, golden brown, and wrapped in a thin white cover?"

He frowned at me.

I waited.

"OK. Think of the bright red hair. What does bright red hair remind you of?"

"A sexy woman. A woman who's hot."

"OK. Good work Bill. So what is thin, golden-brown, wrapped in white, and hot?"

"I haven't a clue."

"Think. Connect more dots. It's your dream and somewhere, deep inside, you know the answer. Take your time. Go over the symbol again."

"Well, a thin, golden-brown something, dressed in a thin white skinny dress, wait, there are no curves, my niece looks like a stick in the dream. There's red hair, no, flaming red hair. That's what I see."

"Hmmm, not pudgy or curvy, but like a stick." I paused. "Good. Keep seeing it, this thin, sticklike, toasty brown thing with red-hot flaming hair. Tie it to the past, to the basement. What comes up?"

Bill stared at the carpet, frowned some more, and then looked up in surprise, almost jumping up in excitement. "Jesus Christ!" he exclaimed. "She's a cigarette! A goddamn cigarette! Damn!" He smiled triumphantly, slapping his knee. "Damn, a cigarette. Damn."

"Good work, Bill! You got it. That's terrific!"

There was another pause while he went into himself and what his interpretation could mean. Meanwhile, I percolated along those same lines. I knew his twentieth sobriety date was coming up, and I knew he associated drinking with smoking. I also learned that day that he began to drink and smoke at the age of twelve, the same age as his niece and the hormones that rage at twelve.

I had a revelation too. I suddenly realized that Bill's

unconscious relapse fears were shared with me when he shared this dream. This dream of relapse. Clinically, anniversary dates are prime relapse times. We both knew that. I began to wonder if Bill was thinking of drinking, so I asked him.

"Bill, pay close attention to what I am going to say next. Please keep an open mind." I paused. "I'm concerned that this is a relapse dream. I need to ask you, are you thinking about drinking again?"

Without batting an eye he straightened up, stuck his chin out, and said, "Look, I've been sober twenty years now. That's a long time. I think I've proved I can handle a drink now and then."

"Really? Have you shared these thoughts with your sponsor?"

"I don't see him much anymore."

"Are you still going to meetings?"

"Once in a while."

We faced off. Knowing the therapeutic relationship was secure I made a decision.

"Now here's the deal Bill. You need to call your sponsor and get your ass to a meeting ASAP. You need to share these thoughts with your sponsor and those that have been there. You've got too much to lose. You'll get really physically ill this time, you're no kid anymore. Think about what you said earlier about throwing up in the laundry tub and being out of your mind." I paused. "Really think about that. As for our work, I'd like you to journal about when you were twelve and see if there is anything else happening today, emotionally, that reminds you of that painful time. As you write, pay attention to your feelings, especially the desire to drink, and make a note of that. Remember too the AA adage of alcohol being cunning, powerful, and baffling. Please trust the process and call me if you need to."

He nervously glanced at his watch, then nodded in assent. He stared at me, possibly wondering what would happen if he did take that celebratory, yet deadly, anniversary drink.

"What?" I asked.

"Is it safe to go to my brother's house Sunday?"

"Absolutely."

There are many elements to consider in a dream such as this. First is the relapse aspect of it and how seductive addictions really are. It also addresses the unconscious itch to return to the addiction that every addict carries within. Next I got a further glimpse of Bill's unhappy childhood and how he began to experiment with two formidable drugs, alcohol and tobacco. I also saw how his parents reacted to him, each in their own way, by leaching confidence out of his young Self. I learned how Bill judged himself by literalizing the dream and his fear of seeing his niece again. Surely his relationship with his brother would suffer if that happened.

The dream and Bill's reaction to it is also a prime example of staying true to the three guiding principles of the Subjective Symbol Immersion Method. To state once again, they are:

1. The dream belongs to the dreamer.
2. Don't literalize the dream. Dreams are symbolic, not literal.
3. Don't moralize a dream. Dreams are neither good nor bad, they just are.

Bill also forgot how important it was to shift gears once he took possession of his dream. His emotional reaction was regressive and he literalized the dream and then judged himself harshly. Both these behaviors challenged his ability to get to his core truth and face his deep, unconscious desire to return to drinking.

Thankfully Bill did not relapse and eventually reconnected with both his sponsor and his regular AA meetings. Last I learned he continues to enjoy Sunday dinners at his brother's house too.

Exercise: Go over Bill's dream and find all the elements discussed in earlier chapters. The story of the dream, the theme of the dream, cast of characters, etc. Circle key questions. You'll find they may be out of synch with the outline but most of them are there. Look at the dialogue. Did Bill answer questions without my asking? Identify Bill's emotional reaction to the dream. What were his feelings? This exercise will help you process your own dream material as we move into more complicated dreams.

CHAPTER IX

Rest and Review

The process is going to get trickier and more challenging from now on, so going back over the SSIM process before we move into the next two dreams and deeper exercises is a good idea.

Remember that this book works with dreams from a mainstream perspective. It is written with the general population in mind and is very hands-on. Everything is boiled down to its essence and then reframed in a user-friendly way eliminating as much psycho-babble as possibly.

If you recall it was best to look at dreams as if we are viewing a play, watching a movie or reading a book. They are often incomplete and SSIM helps us write the third act, final scene, or last few chapters. Remember, dreams are stories that come to us while we sleep. According to Carl Jung, these stories have meaning and purpose. Jung states, "Dreams are . . . natural phenomena which are nothing other than what they present to be. They do not deceive, they do not lie, they do not distort or disguise; they are invariably seeking to express something that the ego does not know and does not understand."

As you've discovered it's hard to understand our dreams because they appear in symbolic form. No one understands why, although many try. For our purposes it doesn't really matter. It just is. We have to accept that and work with that challenge.

Dreams often present a current situation, stimulated by an event we may not be consciously aware of, a situation that either stimulates unfinished emotional business or is pushing us to a new, more complete sense of Self. Whatever the dream is, it needs our attention, especially those that repeat themselves or are part of an ongoing theme, like quest dreams. In addition, the Subjective Symbol Immersion Method presented here is based on personal growth and self-awareness, and adheres primarily to Carl Jung's theory on dreams as messages from our deepest truth.

If you recall Jung believed dreams revealed parts of ourselves we needed to pay attention to in order to be more *fully aware of who we really are (the True Self),* warts and all. We need that in order to have a clear *sense of self-identity*, the foundation of one's emotional life. In addition, Jung believed dreams presented *new points of view,* especially if there was some psychological conflict the dreamer was experiencing, even if unconsciously. Julia's and Bill's dreams certainly bore that out.

To put the word *unconscious* into perspective and show it some respect, it has been determined by the analytical community that barely ten percent of what's going on in our heads is known to us. That makes dreams, their meanings, and all other aspects of the unconscious take up residence in our psyche to the tune of ninety plus percent. That's a lot of psychological real estate! With those stats it is all the more important that we pay attention to dreams and put energy into figuring out their primary symbols.

Remember, Jung said, "The whole dreamwork is essentially subjective, and a dream is a theater in which the dreamer is himself the scene, the player, the prompter, the producer, the author, the public and the critic."

Through SSIM it's been demonstrated through Julia's and Bill's dreams that there is a personal and subjective meaning to dreams. Committing fully to the guiding principle that *the dream belongs to the dreamer* is essential to the process.

I'd like you to carve in stone that no one else can interpret your dream or tell you what it means. The best another person can do is ask the right questions in order to prompt the dreamer to grasp the meaning of the symbol and eventually connect the dots from within his or her unconscious. Remember, once the primary symbol is identified it becomes the lynchpin of the dream and all other elements will in some way connect to it.

Now let's look again at some of the questions that will act as guides to the heart of the dream. It might help if you think of yourself as a writer who has to produce a play, movie, or book using the material from the dream.

- The *Who* of the Dream? (the actors)
    - How old are you in the dream?
    - Who else is in the dream?
- The *Where* of the Dream? (the setting)
    - Where are you in the dream?
    - Is the place familiar?

    - Describe the place in as much detail as you can.
- The *When* of the Dream? (time frame of your play)
    - What time in your life do you think this dream is taking place?
    - If you're younger in this dream, where were you living then?
    - Who was the most important friend in your life back then?
    - What happened to him or her?
    - If the person moved ask about age and loss.
- The *What* of the Dream? (the action)
    - What is the action in the dream?
    - What are the characters doing?
- The *Why* of the Dream?
    - Why do you suppose you're having this dream now?
    - What is happening in your life today that reminds you of that time?

Let's go ahead and use the above outline to work on another one of your dreams. Perhaps you have a Big Dream that haunts you or a repetitive dream you want to explore. Be OK with any dream because for the purpose of practicing and mastering SSIM, any dream will do. If you are the creative type, go for it. Let all your creative juices flow. Rather than write a play, movie or story, perhaps you'll want to paint your dream or create a song or poem around it.

Meanwhile, it's best for the rest of us to stick with the outline and methodically go through it, answering the questions in order. Use SSIM and the basic questions with as many dreams as you wish until you feel a sense of mastery around the method. Go back to the earlier questions and then add the more recent ones to the list. It's all a process that will eventually come full circle for you. It's very important to feel mastery right now. To be comfortable finding the primary symbol and exploring it through all the questions as soon we will be moving on to deeper work with symbols.

If you're still uncertain go back to your Inner Child and picture yourself learning to ride a bike or roller skate. You may be too young to remember but once you didn't know your ABCs and now look, you are reading this book! Cheer yourself on. You *will* master this just like you mastered your ABCs.

If you need to take a break right now to continue processing what you've learned so far, that's fine. After a brief course on Archetypes in the next chapter, the final, deeper work and more complicated dream examples are next.

CHAPTER X

Archetypes

This is a good place to pause and learn about archetypes and why they appear in dreams. Archetypes are part of our psyche. They hang out in the unconscious and strongly influence how we see and experience the world. We can never fully know our influential archetypes or make them fully conscious but we can have a sense of which archetypes influence us by reflecting on some of the decisions we've made in the past and by looking at which ones appear in our dreams.

Jung believed that archetypes are models of people, behaviors, or personalities. We use examples of that all the time. Think of modern archetypes such as Hippie, Nerd, and Rebel. Think about a Biker, then close your eyes. Can't you see the archetype of a Biker whizzing through your mind's eye? Spend some time seeing him. Add as many details as you can. Ask yourself how you feel about the biker. It's a good exercise to do with all the archetypes you discover. I bet you could name a dozen modern archetypes right now. When you really think about it, the list of archetypes is endless. Even cultures have archetypes. Can you name some?

Jung also believed that the psyche not only included the conscious ego and the personal unconscious but something called the *collective unconscious* as well.

The personal unconscious is where we store all our suppressed memories while the collective unconscious is a part of the psyche that functions on a larger scale. Jung looked at it as a container of psychological inheritance that contains all of the buried knowledge and experiences we share as being part of the human condition. Just think of it as a DNA of the mind. The collective unconscious, Jung believed, is where these archetypes exist. He suggested that these models, in the classical sense, are innate, universal, and hereditary. Archetypes such as Mother, The Warrior, The Hero, The Child, and so on are in our very nature and function to organize how we experience certain things. Other archetypes such as the modern ones mentioned earlier can be learned as they culturally develop and then become personally integrated.

"All the most powerful ideas in history go back to archetypes," Jung explained in his book *The Structure of the Psyche*. "This is particularly true of religious ideas, but the central concepts of science, philosophy, and ethics are no exception to this rule. In their present form they are variants of archetypal ideas created by consciously applying and adapting these ideas to reality. For it is the function of consciousness, not only to recognize and assimilate the external world through the gateway of the senses, but to translate into visible reality the world within us."

In other words we need a container like a stock pot with

a lid that lifts up to allow psychological ingredients in for us to blend with our personal unconscious until they become conscious. Usually these concepts come through education and/or life experience. The important thing to remember is to *stay open to new ideas.* Like spices, they will stimulate you and add flavor to your life.

In the course of his ground breaking theories Jung identified four core archetypes yet believed there were many more. As we have seen the list of archetypes that are classical, historical, and contemporary is endless. Jung's four archetypes are the Self, the Shadow, The Anima/Animus, and the Persona.

The Self is an archetype that represents the coming together of the unconscious and conscious elements of an individual. In other words both parts of your psychological world. The ten percent and ninety percent mentioned earlier. We become unified over time through a process called individuation or maturation, i.e., mastering the challenges and heartbreaks of growing up. Where our parts get integrated into a complete whole as we strive toward our potential. Think of the Circle of Life.

The Shadow represents the part of our psyche that is judged "bad" by us. Sometimes it isn't bad at all, but as children we were taught it was. The Shadow is also a fragment of our primitive self, the self whose only goals are sex and survival. We tend to suppress or bury these fragments leaving them lurking in our unconscious only to pop up and deliver a message in our dreams. Snakes, monsters, devils, dark strangers, lunatics, and other terrifying creatures all represent the Shadow. If you have one of these images in your dream ask yourself what part of your Shadow is showing up now and why. Remember dreams are our best friends and introduce us to our Shadows *only when we're ready to deal with them.*

Finally, the most important reason to embrace your Shadow is that is contains a terrific amount of energy and, like a diamond under extreme pressure, will transform into a dazzling light, illuminating other parts of the Self for you to embrace. When that happens you will be amazed at how your Shadow suddenly becomes a gift to you. A gift of an invaluable, life affirming, creative resource.

- The Anima and Animus can be tricky. Think of them as how you may truly experience men and women on the deepest level of your psyche. Trust that there's an overarching, timeless, universal belief about genders and gender archetypes that all of us unconsciously adhere to. A well-rounded psyche has the ability to tap into the energy of *both* genders if necessary. The Mother (Feminine) can tap into her Inner Warrior (Masculine) to fight for her family and her beliefs. The Warrior can be tender and nurturing if the situation requires it.

We often hear terms such as the "feminine side" and "male energy." Those terms come from our recognition of both genders within the human psyche. In addition the Greek gods and goddesses acted as role models for feminine and masculine perceptions. Whatever qualities you impose on them understand those qualities are reflections of your unconscious anima and animus who represent parts of who you truly are. Finally, together they represent totality and wholeness.

The Persona is how we present ourselves to the world. The word *persona* comes from a Latin word that means "mask." We all have many Personas. The one we wear to school, work, church, etc., and the one we wear to parties, while on vacation, or on a first date. Trust that there is a Persona for every social occasion. We need them to not only shield us from the harm of ego wounds delivered regularly by our outside worlds, but to survive in a very complicated, media driven social system. Jung believed the Persona appeared in dreams and wore many different masks. The next time you are out and about socially pay attention to what Persona you have worn for the occasion, then look at the Personas you wear in your dreams, the ones you don't consciously know about.

A good example of this is Tom's dream which we'll explore in the next chapter on archetypes as primary symbols. Tom dreamed of his childhood friend Mike and Mike's mom. Two popular primary Archetypes, the Child and the Mother.

Bill's dream had an archetype in it too. Remember the alluring red head? That Archetype is called the Seductress or Siren. It's very possible that Bill would not have paid attention to that life-saving dream if the image hadn't been "hot" and raised sexual feelings in him. We can always trust the dream to give us what we need, when we need it.

Below this you'll find a list of common, classical archetypes other than those mentioned above and the characteristics they represent that appear in dreams. They can be of both genders. See if you can spot some of them in your dreams or in the dreams of others. That will be good practice for you as you strive to uncover your True Self, Shadow and all.

- Mother—nurture, comfort, care.
- Father—authority, power, stability.
- Child—rebirth, salvation, innocence, playfulness.
- Hero—rescue, defend, save, champion.
- Wise Elder—knowledge, wisdom, guidance, experience.

- Trickster—deception, trouble, manipulation.
- Faceless Man or Woman—unknown parts of Self.
- "Puer" (childish adult male)—boyishness, immaturity, shallowness.
- Maiden, Young Girl or Virgin—innocence, desirability, purity, naïveté.
- Rebel-anger, rebellion, challenge—freedom.
- Jester or Clown—truth cloaked in wit, distraction, levity.
- Seductress—beautiful, sexy, alluring, dangerous.
- Companion or Spirit Guide—mentor, caretaker, protector.
- Anonymous Crowd—usually represents the community and its values.
- Warrior—battle, attack.
- Vampire—death, intrigue, danger.

A good exercise would be to watch *The Wizard of Oz* as many archetypes appear in that film. Another great film that makes a point of presenting archetypes is *The Breakfast Club.* Can't you just see the Rebel, the Jock, the Nerd, the Weirdo, and the Princess from that film right now? See if you too can identify them.

Another good exercise is to start a list of contemporary archetypes like the Yuppie, the Nerd, and the Foodie. There are so many. Make a list and see if you can identify characteristics of the modern archetypes on your list. Fun!

CHAPTER XI

The Primary Symbol as an Archetype—Tom's Dream

Often childhood friends appear in dreams. Most people scratch their heads and wonder why someone they haven't seen in years appears while they sleep. Usually, the dream is dismissed because the dreamer can't imagine why. (If suddenly you remember a dream with a childhood friend in it right now, get a pen or pencil, and write it down).

After you read Tom's dream you'll then have all the information you need to work on your own childhood dream figure. If you don't have a childhood-friend dream that pops into your head right now, that's OK, you may someday.

Before you read Tom's dream here is a valuable exercise to help you connect some dots between the processing he did and the work you can do. Not all the questions on this list appear in his dream but most of them do. In addition, some are implied by his expanded answers.

Imagine a friend from your childhood or past appearing in

your dream. You know by now it's important but not exactly how important or why. To help you, here is a list of questions you can ask yourself:

Why that particular friend? ____________________

____

Why now? ________________________________

____

What did that friend mean to you? ______________

____

What kind of person was that friend? ____________

____

What characteristics did that friend have? ________

____

What does he or she symbolize as I look back and reflect on that person? ______________________

____

How did we part? __________________________

____

Why did we part? __________________________

____

Do I have unfinished business with that friend?

____

Did I meet someone recently that reminded me of that friend? ______________________________

This seems like a lot of questions, but just remember how vital all the answers are and how they will give the you the best possible idea of what the symbol and the dream truly means to you.

Finish this exercise by finishing the following sentence:

If I could say one thing to that friend right now, I would say ____

____

____.

Tom's Dream

Years ago a young male client I had been working with for nearly two years told me this dream.

"Last night I dreamed of my childhood friend Mike. It was really weird, we were both kids in the dream, about ten, I would guess. I haven't seen Mike in over ten years. Strange. Why do you think I'm dreaming of him and why are we kids in the dream?"

"Interesting. Now tell me, Tom, where were both of you in the dream?"

"It's not clear. I think we were in a yard. It was grassy, I remember that."

"Good."

Mike was clearly the primary symbol in the dream so I skipped ahead and asked him to tell me about Mike.

"Mike was a great kid. He was smart, funny, kind, and most of all loyal. We were in Scouts together. We competed for badges."

"What else?"

"Well, we competed, we were neck and neck and he got one more badge then I did and won the contest. I was pissed."

I took note here that Tom had used the word *compete* twice in two sentences. This gift from the dream would be useful later in helping him connect the past and the present.

"Hmmm. Competition again. The trader's life." (Tom was a floor trader at the Board of Trade in Chicago.)

"Ain't that the truth," he said with a smile.

"Let's get back to Mike. There's a reason you're dreaming of him now. Keep digging. What happened to your friendship?"

With this question Tom got quiet and looked down at the floor. Sensing turmoil, I waited. He looked up and said, "This is embarrassing."

"OK. Understand but I hope we're past that stage. You've shared some pretty deep stuff with me." I paused for that to sink in. "Tell me."

"Well, to tell the truth, I stole his Cub Scout belt. I didn't have one. His was almost new and the buckle was really shiny. Everyone looked all over for it and no one accused me of stealing it but I think Mike knew." Tom paused, looking down again. "He stopped being my friend then. This great kid I wanted to be friends with forever. I think both our moms knew too, but my mom was too drunk and ashamed to ever confront me."

He went on in a softer voice. "I wanted to be like Mike, I wanted to have Mike's mom be my mom. You know, the kind of mom that's sober when you get home from school. That cooks and bakes and picks you up on time. The mom that shows up at your hockey game. That kind of mom, the opposite of my mom," he said softly, finally looking up at me expectantly.

I had to avoid the "blaming mom trap" in thinking about my response. I knew that wouldn't help Tom grow and accept responsibility for his life. After all he was thirty three. I ignored his silent request and took the therapeutic plunge.

"I hear your sadness, Tom. That's alcoholism, alcoholic behavior, not your mom. Now, let's get back to the dream. You just said you wanted to be like Mike. Tell me, Tom, if you were like Mike today, what would you do differently?"

To my surprise Tom burst out laughing. It wasn't a fun laugh though; it was a snide, bitter laugh. A laugh that could have said, "Are you nuts, lady? Get with it." I waited a bit longer and then decided it was time for tough love.

"What was that about?" I said, not waiting for an answer. "Listen, Tom, you've been coming here for nearly two years. You've spent a lot of time and money. You tell me you want to heal and grow, well here it is, the moment of healing and growth. You can just laugh and be on your way or get real with me. I care about you, but I can't do your healing for you." I waited a few moments, then leaned forward. In a softer tone I said "Tom" then waited. "Go the distance, Tom. It's time."

He shifted in his seat and for a minute I thought he was going to leave. He even started to get up. I thought, "*Oh, no.*" We stared at each other, then just like air escaping from a balloon the energy shifted. He settled back on the couch. He looked at me, then offered a barely noticeable nod.

Face flushed and looking down again he said, "I'd have to change everything if I wanted to be like Mike today. It's overwhelming. I've been a real asshole for a long time. I'm doing things today that Mike would never do. I'm not honest or loyal. I cheat on my wife, steal from my friends, and lie at work. I'm not really even honest here. I don't tell you half the shit that's going on in my head. I scare myself sometimes. Remember your talk about the Shadow? That part of people that no one wants to admit to? Well, I've got a big effing Shadow and I don't know what to do with it. It's killing me. Sometimes, late at night, when I can't sleep, I think about dying. I want to die."

Tom broke down then. His head sunk down even farther, his elbows on his knees, his hands covering his face. I studied his posture and body language. Fundamentally he was a strong, healthy guy whose childhood was ruined by alcoholism, but somewhere, perhaps before his mom fell victim to alcohol, she gave him some of what he needed.

He continued to cry in a quiet, dignified way for such a diamond-in-the-rough guy. I touched his shoulder, handed him a tissue, then waited, honoring the therapeutic value of a good cry. When he calmed down he said, "I mean it, at times I really wanted to die. I even thought about killing myself." I let more time pass staying present in our *temenos*, then suddenly there was another shift of energy in our therapeutic container and I did my intervention.

"Tom, I can understand that. The burden's been tremendous but there's no chance of that now. You just owned your Shadow and now it's in the light. Can't you sense that? Don't you feel lighter, more together? I want you to trust that this is a real moment for you to heal and grow. For you to transform and become Mike's symbolic friend again. The dream is telling you, in a way, you *can* go back again. You can reclaim your true nature, the part of you that connected to a kid like Mike. Remember you had things in common, were good buddies, until your Shadow- *your need to compete and win above all else*- took hold. It's been running your life ever since. That's what's killing you." Still looking down, he nodded. Another shift in the room.

"Tom, I want us to spend the rest of our time together talking about that deep need, that unfillable hole or hunger for love you've been walking around with. It's time to learn winning doesn't equate to love or being loved. I'm guessing your cheating, stealing, and lying all have something to do with competing, with needing to win. Am I right?"

Tom looked up then. Suddenly he appeared ten years younger, runny nose and all. He nodded again. I was relieved and impressed with the inner work he just did. With how he stayed open, no matter how painful it was, to owning his Shadow, the thing that was spiritually killing him. I saw how he was able to be totally honest, to transform, allowing his younger self, through that honesty, to let the boy that was Mike's friend shine through the darkness.

We smiled at each other. His nose was a boyish shade of red. "You've got a deal," he said.

It took Tom a long time to let go of his hunger. To understand someone can be loved even if they lose. This lesson was best driven home by his daughter's gymnastics competition and his son's Little League games.

Later he told me, "At first I was really upset when my kids lost, made mistakes, blew shots. My wife got all over me for that. One night I realized, especially after a big defeat on the parallel bars to my asshole neighbor Bob's kid, that I loved my daughter Mindy even though she lost big time. I loved her with all my heart and knew that she loved me. It was big, knowing that. Really big. Maybe that's what the Mike dream was all about. About kids showing the way." I smiled and nodded in agreement.

This dream was the breakthrough Tom needed to unburden himself from the past, to become authentic, and move on. He completed therapy six months later and three years after that I got an announcement that he had completed his certification to be an advanced substance abuse counselor. He wrote on the back of the announcement that he planned to specialize in alcoholic family systems.

It's important to understand that in Tom's idealized memory of Mike and Mike's mom they were perfect. In reality they were human, thus imperfect like the rest of us, but in Tom's childhood he needed them to be idealized. Why? There are two reasons. The first is he needed to know there was a happy family somewhere in his limited world that accepted him (symbolically) into it. That is how he eased his suffering. The second reason is because only then would his dream have an impact on him. It was the one significant relationship in his childhood that could point the way to deeper healing. Recalling Mike and his mother compelled Tom to act (bringing the dream to me) and eventually strive for the more healed Self he was destined to become (a healer for others).

Mike, as well as being a symbol of Tom's lost innocence, was also the Child archetype in the dream that promised Tom a new beginning. Just think of the New Year's Baby and new beginnings when you think of the Child archetype.

The primary archetype of Mother, on the other hand, symbolized the ability of the psyche to recognize not only where we all come from (even the gods and goddesses had moms), but also a type of relationship we all need, have, and/or seek at one time or another. You've probably heard about or experienced the dark night of the soul? A place of our deepest pain and despair. That's the place where we all cry out for mom. A place where we need unconditional love, comfort, caring, and support. If our own mom fails us we tend to seek another mom and idealize her like Tom did. Mother can be abstract too. For example, as Jung believed, people are part of the collective and for them, Earth Mother is embraced along with Eve, and the Virgin Mary. Even institutions can be maternal archetypes like the corporate Ma Bell (AT&T in the old days) and hospitals like Ma Cook (Cook County Hospital in Chicago). Just look around you, symbolic moms are everywhere!

Now remember the exercise you did before Tom's dream? The one about the childhood friend in your dream? If you haven't done it yet, please do. This is another golden opportunity for you to mind that rich mother lode inside of you.

Finish this exercise by completing the following sentence about your dream:

The part of my friend in the dream that I want to embrace (or not) is:

____

____

____.

CHAPTER XII

Archetypes and Dream Themes

Dream Momma ©

A dream theme is a series of dreams over time where the same symbol or things relating to the same symbol regularly appear. The dream theme reveals itself best if the dreamer keeps a dream journal. In the section titled *The Dreamer's Toolkit* you'll learn how to keep a dream journal. It can take a while for the theme to appear, but over time, sometimes a long time, it will. Often, upon rereading their dream journals dreamers can identify the symbols that repeat themselves and spot the theme. I think of the reoccurring symbol in a dream theme as a thread purposely woven into the fabric of a dream by the unconscious, like Native Americans wove tiny mistakes into their blankets while on the looms. They did this not just as a form of personal identification but to suggest perfection was not part of the human condition and all humans were prone to error.

I had a client whose dream theme was a white horse

that appeared randomly in her dreams over a period of three months. When we pulled the thread it led to a knot tied around a childhood rocking horse destroyed when her father was in a drunken rage. My client was just young enough to believe in magical thinking and thought her little rocking horse was real. She remembered naming it Pepper because it was white with tiny black dots on its rump. She fed it real carrots. The experience of seeing her "pet" destroyed deeply traumatized her.

Children as young as Pepper's little mistress know instinctively that in order to survive they need their parents or caregivers so they go into denial and bury early traumas they experience at their hands. Years later the traumatic experiences often trickle up to consciousness through dreams when the adult is strong enough psychologically to emotionally handle them. Once they do, they can work on healing in therapy, self-help, journaling, etc. Whatever path to wholeness they choose.

The Shadow archetype is so pervasive and such a stealth operator that it's nearly impossible to tease it out through conscious methods. Most often we see the Shadow in someone's behavior. They act or do something that may raise an eyebrow or two. Other times the Shadow is experienced as a feeling about someone. You may feel "there's something off about that guy" or sense a mean streak in a woman. Other times you might think someone is "too good to be true," as they often are. It is aptly named, as it's very, very tricky to spot the Shadow. It's even harder to spot your own Shadow.

Here is a brief story about a woman who recognizes her

Shadow and transformed her relationship with her daughter because of it. She told me this dream.

"I had a dream that there was a crazy woman in the kitchen of my house. She had a butcher knife and was chasing my daughter around the kitchen table. I ran into the kitchen, grabbed my daughter, and hid her under the steps leading upstairs. Then I ran back into the kitchen to deal with this crazy woman but she wasn't there anymore."

She went on to say, "When I told my daughter Cindy about this dream we both laughed, but then she said something that stuck like a burr. She said, 'I bet you wish sometimes she had caught me.' I realized Cindy was right. She's been driving me crazy with all that weird blue hair of hers and those sneaky tattoos and piercings she thinks I don't know about. At times I do want to kill her!" Recognizing the Frustrated Mom archetype, we both laughed.

"I don't blame you, she's a handful, but very creative and smart too. It's interesting to me that she saw your Shadow so you could see it too. Good for her! Now it's in the light and you can both laugh about it."

"I love my daughter."

"I know you do. That's why you went back into the kitchen to do battle with your Shadow and poof, just like that, it was gone and transformed into light."

I'd like you to think about the Shadow in your psyche. Think about the negative traits you notice in others and then ask yourself if you have those same traits, even a little bit. Go back over your dreams and see if you can spot a Shadow archetype lurking around, like the crazy woman or a dark stranger. Once you can identify your Shadow it too will transform into light and, just like the sun bathing the Earth with solar power, your true Self or Soul will feel energized too. You'll know the transformation from dark to light has taken place because you'll feel more alive, more energetic, more empowered, more *authentic.* Next, you'll see how drilling down to the heart of one's Shadow can be so transformative through Amanda's dreamwork.

CHAPTER XIII

The Shadow Transformed—Amanda's Dream

"Dear Dream Momma, I've been reading your dream blogs and hope you can help me. For as long as I can remember I've been having dreams about vampires. In my earlier years they've been horrible, mindless creatures that I desperately ran from, not in fear of death, but in fear of being turned into a vampire. However the older I got, the calmer my reaction to the dreams became. They turned even pleasant. Now they are sensual, beautiful dreams! I'm charmed by incredibly attractive male vampires, and if in the beginning of the dream I am reluctant to fall into the temptation, in the end I always find myself in bed with the once horrible creatures and am head over heals in love with them. I am becoming the vampire I once dreaded. Please help! I've been trying to get this figured out for years, and I don't really want to be a predator. What can I do?"

I replied as best I could given the dream content and urged her to get help. Apparently what I said hit the mark on some level because the dreamer, a young woman from Tampa, Florida, named Amanda (an alias) called me a few months later. She asked if she could come in for a dream consultation and to follow up on her letter to me. She hoped to end "once and for all" her "haunting dreams." I was very happy she wanted to follow through and agreed to see her.

After we worked together I realized her dreams were repetitive or reoccurring dreams that nagged her with her own self-loathing in the form of her Shadow Archetype, the Vampire.

Amanda's dream is also a good example of what happens when the Shadow takes root in one's unconscious and begins a life of its own. The dream exemplified the seeds of many things non-spiritual or Shadow-like that occur in a toxic household. Things like broken trust, boundary violations, contemptuous behavior, secrets, cruelty, jealousy, and the like. But worst of all it can be the horror of someone becoming the thing once feared and loathed.

Later, during our session, Amanda went on to say, "I'm very conflicted about these dreams. Part of me hates that the once horrible creature is now my lover and the other part doesn't want to let go. I need to tell you that in the most recent dream my vampire lover is not so attractive anymore. Please help me. I'm tired of worrying about it and I just don't get it. What does all this mean?"

Amanda and I agreed that the primary dream symbol was the archetype of the Vampire so we went right into coaxing out the unconscious meaning of the Vampire and her response to him. I told her that if we worked together I was confident we could make sense of it all and that the vampire dreams would end once she brought that shadow aspect of her unconscious into the light. I explained to her that the guiding principle would be the dream belongs to the dreamer and I gave her material to understand and to study the Subjective Symbol Immersion Method we would use. Soon our work began.

"Amanda, do you remember when the vampire dreams started?"

"Not really. My mom told me I had a lot of nightmares as a little kid. A toddler. Maybe they started then. I really can't remember."

"OK, that's fine. Now think about what you remember, not what Mom told you. It's important that we work with your dream recall."

"OK. Well then I'd have to say, for as long as I can remember."

"OK. How far back can you remember? Kindergarten? Pre-school age? Try to narrow it down a bit. It's important."

"I'll try." Amanda paused and looked over my head out the window to the lake beyond. "I'm going to say about three, maybe four years old. I remember I was still in my crib but it was lower and the side was down. I remember my mom coming to comfort me."

"Good. That's very good. Thanks, that gives us a good starting point. When was the last dream?"

"Just a week ago. It was very sensual."

"Sensual, but not scary?"

"Well, more sensual than scary. I'm scared of them when I wake up but in the dream I'm not scared at all."

"OK. So to be perfectly clear, now they aren't really scary?"

"Not anymore, but they just keep coming back. I'm feeling held back somehow. I'm feeling there's something there but can't imagine what it could be. That's why I'm here. "

"OK. We'll work it out. Now let's move on with our time line. How often do they occur?"

Amanda was thoughtful for a while. I sensed how hard she was working to help me help her. It felt good to have our work become collaborative.

"It's hard to say. I'd say every other month or so," she replied.

"Every other month since three or four years of age? Are you sure?"

"I've had them as far back as I can remember."

"Amanda, that's a lifetime of reoccurring dreams. Had you never, ever once, thought about exploring them?"

"I did buy a symbol book once, but remember being either confused or frustrated. Nothing seemed to fit."

I tried not to groan out loud. "Did you by any chance keep a diary or dream journal about them?"

"It's funny you should ask. When I got older, I did. It was when I was about eleven or twelve, when they got less scary." She looked at me very earnestly then. "I was afraid if I wrote them down earlier they would be more real and then I'd lose it and upset my mom."

"You seem to feel a need to protect your mom. Let's look at that later. OK?"

"I'd like that."

"Now, is it fair to say that your sensual feelings overcame your fearful ones? Is that why the dreams became less scary?"

"Well, yes, and honestly, sexual is a more accurate word."

"OK. Let's be very clear here as sensual and sexual can mean different things to different people. I need specific examples."

Amanda paused at this point, avoiding eye contact with

me. She was clearly experiencing shame. I realized it was intervention time. I spoke softly.

"Amanda, please hear me about this one very, very important fact. Dreams like yours are always symbolic in nature. Sex, sex acts, sexual behavior and all of that are not to be taken literally or as fact. There are exceptions of course, but please trust me on that. OK?"

"They seem so real. Sometimes I wake up all excited. If they're not to be taken as fact why do I wake up all hot and bothered?"

"That's a good question. The best answer is that our body has a mind of its own. When stimulated it goes into action without our mind having anything to do with it. For example, you get a mosquito bite that itches. You don't think about it and say to yourself, 'gee I have a mosquito bite I think I'll scratch it with my nails for ten seconds,' do you?"

"No, of course not," she replied, smiling.

"OK. Then just understand that your body, when stimulated by sexual images, reacts the same way. It's normal and nothing to be ashamed of. Your body doesn't know these images are symbolic."

"Really?"

"Absolutely. You'll have to trust me on that." I paused and we both held eye contact for a moment, then her face relaxed. I smiled and asked her, "Are you ready to get on with your dreams now?"

"Absolutely!" She smiled and sat straighter.

We plodded away together, our goal being to understand the symbolic nature of her vampire dreams. I had some pet theories about them but stuck to my belief that the dream belongs to the dreamer and kept silent. I understood that the issue behind the vampire dreams was very complex and would take time. Many months went by while other, more immediate issues went under the microscope. However, like prospectors sensing gold we always went back to digging away at the vampire dreams. Then one day, pay dirt! Amanda showed up, her face pale, a slight tremble to her lips.

"Amanda, what's going on? Are you OK?"

"No. No, I'm not." She stumbled toward the couch.

I took her arm to steady her, then took her hand and held it. "Tell me."

"I had another vampire dream, a bad one. This dream wasn't sexy and fun it was terrifying. In this dream my once desirable and handsome vampire turned grotesque, like the picture of Dorian Gray, and began chasing me with a knife. I screamed in the dream and out loud too. I woke up covered in sweat, my heart pounding. It was awful."

Amanda and I sat quite still, both of us churning away at this abrupt shift in her dream experience. I recalled my earlier fears and with her hands over her face she was quietly weeping.

"Amanda, I can't decide for you, but if you want to use this time to just be with your feelings, I'm OK with that. Or if you want to begin looking at what this shift might mean, I'm OK with that too. It's your call."

Time crawled by and eventually Amanda looked up and gave me a wan smile. "I'm OK. It's time. As weak as I must look, I feel pretty strong inside. Part of me has been preparing for some type of shift or breakthrough. I think this is it so I'd like to move forward."

I smiled back. "You know, Amanda, suddenly our baby

steps have turned into a leap into the abyss. It's normal to be scared."

"With you as a lifeline, I'd like to jump in."

"Let's go. I'm right beside you. Let me ask you this, how old were you in this latest dream?"

"I'm not sure, but I felt younger than I am now."

"OK. Good. We'll look at this now so try to relax and let your memory do some work for you. OK?"

Amanda did some voluntary deep breathing and was able to relax. She scowled a lot, but I took that to mean she was searching, trying to connect some dots between her memory and the dream. I asked her what the primary symbol in this latest dream was and she said it was the knife. After more prodding and asking her to describe the knife, she told me it was more like a scalpel than a regular kitchen knife or "bad guy" knife. She seemed agitated. Amanda's father was a surgeon and I realized that her alarm indicated she had made that connection too.

"It's time to tell me more about your father, Amanda."

"I'm not sure I can."

"You have to. We're already in the abyss and it's time. Trust that you're ready to push through this. You're here. I'm here. You haven't flipped out or done anything foolish. It's time to trust yourself. I trust you." She nodded.

"My dad was a complicated man. He was a control freak and a workaholic. As early as I can remember I sensed he had a cruel streak in him. Nothing I can pinpoint now as an adult but something I just sensed. I was afraid of him for as long as I can remember. He did weird things."

"Like what? It's helpful at this point to be detailed."

"Well, when he was home, which wasn't very often, he

used to tuck me in at night but instead of reading me a favorite story he would tickle me until it hurt. That made my mom pretty mad but I don't remember her stopping it. Once he even pinched me really hard then quickly turned the light out, kissed me on the forehead, and said 'Good night, baby.' It was almost as if the pinch never happened. I remember lying there wondering if I had imagined it but knew I hadn't when I saw the bruise on my arm the next day."

"Did you tell your mom?"

"No, I never did. She was so happy when Dad was home that I didn't want to cause trouble. Spoil it for her."

"That's quite a sacrifice Amanda. Was Mom that fragile?"

"I certainly thought so then. After Dad died she turned into a tiger but back then she seemed very dependent on him. Adored him. I realize now she obeyed him and their relationship was more like master and slave. She was probably afraid of him too." Amanda choked up when she realized this truth. "He never let her forget in subtle ways that he married down."

"OK. Good. Very, very good. Hang in there. You're doing great. Now I have to ask this next question so trust me that it is the next right question to ask. OK?"

She looked alarmed but nodded her assent.

"Did your father ever molest you in any way?"

"I've been waiting for you to ask that. The answer is no, not physically. Not really."

"Tell me what you mean."

"Well, as I grew older I would catch my dad peeking at me when he thought I wasn't looking. He would buy me great clothes and then want me to change into them while he was there. At first I did but after my friend Chris told me that was weird I stopped."

"Good for Chris. What else?"

"More than once he wandered into the bathroom when I was in the shower and a few times I caught him peeking through the crack in the bathroom door. When I was younger he walked around the house nude and never closed the bathroom door when he went but as I got older Mom put a stop to that. It was crazy that for such a big house we only had one full bathroom upstairs."

Once Amanda started she was on a roll. She clearly needed to purge so I was silent.

"Dad wouldn't allow locks on any doors. He said families shouldn't have secrets from one another, and more than once I caught him in my room. I knew he read my diary so I started keeping it in my locker at school. He asked too many questions. Personal questions. Things about my period, stuff like that."

"What did your mom say?"

"I think she thought, like everybody else except Chris, that because he was a doctor those questions were OK. He used his profession a lot to justify a lot of sick behavior, like examining my breasts for lumps. I see now how sick he really was."

We spent many sessions talking about Amanda's relationship with her parents, primarily her dad. What she described, and I believed her, was an intrusive, cruel, passive/seductive father who couldn't keep his boundaries with his daughter. The passive/seductive personality is very subtle, always flying low under the radar. Her father's behavior is a good example. The maddening part about this character flaw is the person who has it doesn't know it and would scream denial all day long if confronted. In addition, Amanda's father was handsome, rich, and admired by the community. Little Amanda never stood a chance and having a child's vulnerabilities, she eventually fell into his shadowy world. A world where, like a vampire, he sucked the innocence and joy out of her. In addition, like all daughters, she had unexpressed romantic feelings for her father despite his personality disorder. A healthy dad would have helped her build strong boundaries. A healthy, less passive and fearful mom would have helped her too. It was like her mom's life was sucked dry too.

Since this was such a breakthrough session for Amanda she wanted to mine it for its far-reaching implications. She understood that the Vampire was a small but very powerful piece of her and that it contained not just the toxic components of her parents (cruel, passive/seductive father and dependent, passive mother) but had drained her of her freedom and cast a shadow over her life.

The first warning bell signaling deep change was when her dream transformed from pleasurable to terrifying. It was as if her unconscious, sensing her newly found ego strength, raised the stakes while at the same time signaling a new beginning for her. It warned both of us that there was rough seas ahead in the form of her finally "telling" the family secrets. A telling that needed to be told but carried within it the elements of betrayal most family victims carry within. For Amanda it was a terrifying yet liberating breakthrough. She knew on a very deep level that her abandonment and banishment fears had vanished. That the feeling of being held back by fear was gone. She didn't need to idealize her parents anymore to emotionally survive. She recognized that it was time to begin her personal journey to the far shore.

When we talked about the something that she felt was there but couldn't imagine what it was I suggested it might be her True Self. The person she was meant to be. When that discussion opened up it led to a whole revelation about the kind of men she had been with (passive/aggressive and cruel) and how she protected her own future children by not marrying one of them. "Suddenly," Amanda joked, "nice guys aren't finishing last." Finally, like many children from toxic families she feared being like her father (there's that Shadow again!) and seriously considered not having children.

I explained to her that the Vampire archetype was a symbol of her spiritual death. Since she had to survive her childhood she had internalized or unconsciously taken into her psyche a parental introject (a part of the parent, in this case her father, that becomes a fraction of the victim's psyche, like a splinter, infecting to some degree all other parts). The good news is, once these Shadow parts are recognized they get transformed through integration into the person's Self *and their powerful energy gets transformed into a positive force.* This is done through letting go of the psychological pressure that's been spent keeping the Shadow contained so the person can feel better about him or her self.

Naturally the dreams never came back and soon it was time for Amanda to steer her own little ship through the waters of life. Last I heard she was staying the course, engaged to a nice guy and doing just fine. In addition to the story of becoming the thing one once dreaded Amanda's dream is an example of how a dream can trigger deep therapeutic work after the dream is understood. Work that is challenged by the dreamer's interpretation of the sexual nature of a dream. Amanda had literalized and judged herself which made it harder for her to see beyond the Vampire to her internalized father. She thought she was the Vampire and on some small level she was but she wasn't stuck with that. She didn't understand about fragments, introjects, and all the other complicated components that make up the psyche. Most importantly she didn't know how to banish or neutralize that vampire energy. She felt doomed and destined to be a predator. Only when she shed light on her family secrets did the Shadow fade. In the telling of her childhood story all shadows emerged. Her father's cruelty, her mother's fear, her childhood shame, everything. Imagine what it must have been like for her to shed that dense, dark cloak of the victim/predator and start a new life.

CHAPTER XIV

The Hero's Journey Peter's Dream

It is important to remember that personal growth is always about choices. For example, embrace versus do battle, lie or tell the truth, marry or remain single, etc. None of us can dictate to another what choices to make. We all have only one road and that is the road we choose to travel. On our road there are many byways. Some are clearly marked by society standards such as education, work, marriage, and family, usually in that order. Yet there is always the road less traveled as choice for all of us. In spite of choices, life can get in the way, it is so hard to predict things but fortunately we are all born with an inner compass called instinct and the more we listen to our "gut" the better our choices in life will be. Our instincts can help us with the hidden Shadow choices people make that are not apparent at first. Those people who trigger a confusing response in many of us. John Doe seems like a great guy but turns out to be a wife beater. Jane Doe is lovely but can't cope with having children and becomes a neglectful mom.

In addition, our gut instincts often appear symbolically in dreams. The dream becomes a wake-up call to get going and resolve whatever it is that needs resolution. Usually the dream and dream symbol appear at a time when something in our current world has triggered a memory and/or we are psychologically strong enough to take it on. Dreams are definitely a call to action. Now, I am not talking about an everyday or garden variety of dream but a *big* dream (one that haunts you) or a repetitive dream (one that nags you like a good mom).

Finally, it is important to understand that many choices are made as compensations for elements missing in our childhood, elements like consistent parenting, an available, nurturing caretaker, loyal friends, etc. For many that have those missing elements, the choices are not really choices made from free adult will, but from childhood needs that never got met. This is another reason it is so important to look at dreams, dream symbols, and archetypes as symbols.

Peter roared up to my home office on a Harley, no helmet, dark hair flying, black leather pants and jacket well worn. He was a new client, a fellow therapist, who told me on the phone he was from "a damaging family who meant well."

Our first session was spent with him saying, "Excuse me?" or "Could you speak a little louder?" for the first twenty minutes. I finally said, "Peter, stop. This isn't going to work if you can't hear me."

I learned that Peter had been a rock band devotee sitting as close as he could to 50,000+ watt speakers every chance he got. By thirty he was nearly deaf. After discussing some options it was decided he would consider hearing aids and come back if he wished. I really didn't expect to see him again. Then one day he called, "I really need help. I'll be getting my hearing aids next week. Can I see you the week after?"

"I have an opening that Wednesday at two if you can make it."

"I'll be there," he said, and that was that.

It was a pleasant Wednesday in April when Peter roared back into therapy to stay for six years. He was a significant passage person in my professional life. He brought me my first client dream and pushed me to help him figure it out. It was a brief dream about me sitting on a hilltop with white sage in my hand. He said I looked like a wise elder. I remember telling him I knew nothing about dreams. I think I asked him to look it up and get back to me so we could talk about it. He refused. Finally I agreed to "look into it" and found myself at the Jung Institute in Evanston, IL.

The second dream, the transformative dream Peter brought to our session a few months later triggered his Hero's Journey and is a sample of the power of a dream fragment to totally transform a life. It was preceded by a simple request. He asked me to help him plan a Vision Quest, something I had done for another client in the same advanced therapy group Peter was in. A Vision Quest is a Native American rite of passage where the male youth of the tribe undergo a challenging ritual designed both as a separation from boyhood and to determine the new role the youth will have in the tribe. Fasting and surviving the wilderness for weeks at a time is intended to bring on the vision. It is believed that the vision and the wilderness experience prophesizes the youth's future. For example, if the young man outruns a deer in his vision he may be named Outruns a Deer and given the role of a hunter or advanced scout.

"You can't just plan a Vision Quest," I stated. "There needs to be some spiritual calling involved. It's not like going on vacation."

"I really want to do it. What do I need to do?"

"Wait. Wait for a calling, or a sign, or something."

"I'm not waiting forever," Peter replied. "I can just start out and see what happens."

"Yes." I agreed. "You can if you think that will work."

A few months later he called between sessions, something he had never done before.

Alarmed, I asked "What's wrong?"

"Nothing, It's good. I had a dream last night. A dream about a map of a small town in Wisconsin. This is about my Vision Quest, I just know it."

"Sounds possible. What are you going to do?"

"I'm driving up there this weekend to check it out. See you next session." And off he went. I was happy for him. He worked hard on himself and although still estranged from his family, did talk occasionally to his oldest sister in spite of her being the one who locked him in the closet as a young child. He deserved this gift.

Having been to Wisconsin often I tried to imagine where a good Vision Quest location would be. Probably way north I remember thinking.

Peter could barely contain his excitement at our next session. He came in waving a Wisconsin map with a broad smile on his face. He pointed to an area within a penciled circle saying, Here, look here. Here it is!" I squinted and peered at the name of an obscure town in upper Wisconsin and smiled.

So plans for a modified Vision Quest were afoot. Peter was going to bone up on the basic requirements for this rite of passage, get the necessary supplies, take a week off from work, and go. He planned to leave in two weeks.

"When I was up there I saw this river with a bunch of people canoeing. I think I'll start my Vision Quest in a canoe. Paddle upriver, find a landing, and hike into the woods."

"Have you ever canoed before?"

"No, no," he said, waving his hand as if shooing away a fly. "How hard can it be? I see kids do it all the time. I'll rent one for a week. It'll be fine."

Hmmm. I thought about Peter's urban lifestyle. I reminisced about my canoeing days near Ely, Minnesota, glanced down at my hands, remembering the blisters that popped up. I was thinking of saying something then decided not to. After all, Peter was a grown man and this was his journey. He agreed to call me just before launching the canoe and also to tell the rental place his plan, just in case. He was gone three days when the phone rang. The caller identified himself as Bert, "Bert from up north, from the canoe place."

"Is he OK?" I asked.

"Well Ma'am, he's got a little problem. Like he can't move 'cause his back went out the first afternoon while paddling upriver. Doris, from Reddings Landing, a ways down the river, found his, I mean, our canoe stuck in some willow reeds with him prostrate on the bottom, his legs draped over the front seat. Don't know how he drifted past us and the whole town but drifted he did, probably at night, the town beds early, you know." He paused "Nothin" about this was our fault. It's a good canoe, one of our best, so no danger of sinking or anything like that."

There was another pause and just before I replied Bert said, "And, oh Ma'am, there's one other thing. He was able to reach his water bottle but while he was lying helpless in the canoe, some local critters ran off with his food so he's pretty hungry. We gave him some crackers, 'cause, you know, it's not good to feed a starving man." I heard a breath followed by a third pause "He's pretty bit up too, skeeters and black flies are fierce this time of year."

As miserable as I pictured him I immediately recognized his experience as a necessary rite of passage and the beginning of his Hero's Journey. It was also a gift. The gift of experiencing the results of ego inflation and also learning one's physical limits.

"Where is he now?"

"At the clinic ma'am. Covered with calamine and loaded with painkillers I imagine." There was an awkward silence. I thought, *Well, he's landed in a temenos (safe container) and will certainly be processing his experience.* Another gift and opportunity.

"Thanks for letting me know."

"Well, that's what he wanted and we aim to please our customers," he said with finality.

It was a humble, more serious Peter who appeared a few weeks later. The three following sessions were focused on his age, physical condition, his self-image and most importantly his learning experience. Peter understood that he was no longer the rock-concert-going biker, doing bongs all night and feeling no pain the next day. "It flew like a blur," he commented. Glimpsing back to my own youth I could only nod in agreement.

In addition we both felt bad. The Vision Quest model I prided myself on didn't work for Peter and although he took some hard reality hits, there were lessons about limits, denial, and self-care learned in the experience. He did battle with his Inner Puer (a Jungian term for eternal youth), then eventually did a visualization and journaled about helping what he called "my Inner Kid" grow up. Eventually he could laugh about it, especially, "the fat little squirrel that stole most of my food, twitching his tail and nose at me, just out of reach. I wanted to strangle that little s--t."

We moved on. One day the phone rang. It was Peter, he was all excited. "It didn't go bad after all."

"What?" I replied.

"The map dream, the Vision Quest. You're not going to believe this."

"Tell me."

"I was telling my oldest sister about the dream, my trip up north, and my back going out and when I mentioned the town she freaked out. She said I was too young to remember, about three when he died, but my grandfather was buried in that town. In a pauper's grave. My dad's dad. She said he was the town drunk. I knew he was a drunk like my dad, but didn't ever know he was in this country and was buried only a day's drive from Chicago." He choked a bit then said, "No one went to the funeral. That really sucks."

"Yes, it does." We both had a moment, honoring death. "What are you going to do?"

"I'm going back up there of course. I'm going to tear those yokel courthouse records apart until I find out something more about him. I want to find his grave. That kind of stuff."

"Call me when you get back," I replied, thinking once again about his hero's journey. And he did.

"It's been a trip. A real trip and an emotional one," Peter said. "I've been all over the place. Went back up north, found the records, grilled my sister Cleo, and learned my grandpa had a big family back in Lithuania. Lots of brothers and sisters, cousins, the whole nine yards. I'm really pissed at my dad for not telling me we had all these people back there. Anyway, dug into the records, puny as they were, and found some emigration info. Traced it back to Ellis so I went to New York to dig some more."

"That's quite a story Peter. I'm impressed. What about work?"

"I'm blowing that off for now. Took a leave. The gig will either be there when I'm done or not. I'm OK with whatever happens. Have some bread to tide me through."

"What happened in New York?"

"Thank God no pencil-pusher messed with our real name. That came later after my parents thought they were better than everyone else. What a joke. Anyway, after a million calls I found someone here, in the States I mean, who had been back there. She's writing me a letter in her native language to introduce me to my family."

I heard Peter's voice crack. "I'm happy for you, Peter. It appears your Hero's Journey continues on after all and that is really exciting to discover."

"Yeah, it feels that way. You know what I keep thinking about?"

"What?"

"That map dream. Remember?"

"How could I not, what with the Vision Quest and all."

"Velva, I never told you but the map wasn't a modern map. I ran out and bought one after the dream. The map in the dream had all the right info but it was parchment-like and kind of frayed around the edges. Brownish."

"Well, that explains a few things. I remember we were so focused on the Vision Quest and your Hero's Journey we didn't really mine the dream for details. My mistake."

"It all worked out after all," Peter replied.

"Well, yes, but it doesn't sound like it's over. What's next for you? Want to come in? Closure is always a good thing, especially after seven years."

"When I come back."

"Come back?"

"I'm flying to Lithuania next week. I'll be in touch. Promise."

A few months later I received a thick letter postmarked from Vilnius, the capital of Lithuania. I stared at it a while, feeling the heft of it in my hand, then opened it.

Dear Velva,

I dreamed about you last week and have been writing this letter on and off since then. I didn't know where or how to begin, I'm not much of a letter writer so I'm starting from the top.

Over here people can hang in the gate area so, when I got off the plane, I noticed a crowd of well-wishers, some carrying flowers, all smiling, waiting at the gate. I never imagined they were waiting for me, but they were. I still choke at the memory. An old guy stepped forward (My great uncle Marius) and stuck out his hand, awkward like. I realized later he really wanted to hug me. He said something to a young girl behind him and she translated, saying, "He knew who you were immediately. He says you look like your grandfather."

I couldn't help it, I laughed and cried at the same time. They laughed and cried too. Suddenly I had a dozen arms around me, everyone smiling and babbling in Lithuanian. I remember breathing in their foreign smells and hugging back. I tried to touch as many of them as I could. I closed my eyes.

A feast was waiting and there were many toasts, most of which I couldn't understand. We drove caravan like for a long time. The house we went to would not be where I stayed. They wouldn't dream of my being in a hotel or inn so I stayed with my second, third? Cousin Antanas who was a student and bi-lingual. His place was almost a dump but to me it was perfect. Homey. A make-shift bed was set up in a corner with a red flowered curtain for privacy. The john was down the hall. (You're going to love this part. Antanas loves to canoe and wanted to take me out the first chance we got.)

I could write forever about what I did and saw but I know you want the meat so here it is.

My grandfather left or fled, I'm not sure which, Lithuania with the intention of working hard and sending for everyone, one at a time. He was, like me, the youngest of five and by all accounts the most fiery and ambitious (not like me). He left amid great fanfare and for a while did send money back. Then he met my grandmother and everything changed. He stopped writing and sending money and only rumors traveled back. Rumors that he had gotten married, started a family, and worked in a factory in Chicago. Later the family heard he had lost his job, found another and lost that too. Then nothing.

I thought, him being a boozer, that all made sense. There are a lot of missing pieces that will have to wait. I met someone.

She is everything to me. Her name is Daila and we spend our free time teaching each other our native languages. She works and has a son. The father is long gone. I am determined to marry her and bring both of them back with me. I don't care how long it takes or what I have to do. My family here supports this. They are thrilled for both of us. Hopefully the wedding will be here and I'm working on making sure it is legal in the States.

I wrote my sister but haven't heard back. It was quite a while ago.

I will keep in touch.

Peter

PS. I did have a dream I want to tell you. I dreamed I was at a train station and when my luggage was unloaded from the baggage car it was encrusted with jewels. Pretty cool huh?

Peter never came back for closure. He did call to tell me he and Daila and her son were living in a Milwaukee suburb and he had a child "of my own." A daughter he named Marion, after his great-grandfather whose name was Marionis. He said they both worked at a nearby hospital. He as a medical social worker (which he was when we met) and she as a tech. He doesn't see much of his family here but keeps in close contact with what he calls his "real family back home." He is at peace with his past and with a smile in his voice told me he canoes all the time now.

As I reflected about Peter and his Hero's Journey I realized a number of things fell into place that made his transformation possible. First, he trusted me and the process. He saw me as both a Wise Woman and surrogate mom. Secondly, unlike the first time when he couldn't hear he was ready for his transformation.

When I sent him away to begin to take care of himself by getting hearing aids (something he secretly knew he needed to do) he began his journey to wholeness. A small, but vital step forward that opened his mind and unconscious up to the Hero's Journey he eventually took. Remember, like a Vision Quest, the Hero's journey is about a search for self-identity and wholeness, a need to do battle both within and without, and a reward at the end. In Peter's case the reward was not only the princess in the form of Daila but a true sense of belonging to a loving family and the personal fulfillment of having children and the legacy they will carry for him. His own "kingdom" so to speak.

Finally, Peter's therapeutic journey truly exemplified the power of a dream and dream symbol, when taken seriously, to transform a life. Peter truly believed in our relationship (as demonstrated by the Wise Woman dream) and the therapeutic process. He took his dreams seriously and understood what a BIG dream was. He immediately recognized the map (symbol) in the dream as important and a call for action. He answered the call and began his Hero's Journey with a trip to northern Wisconsin, then a trip in a canoe, then a trip to NY and Ellis Island, culminating in a trip to Lithuania and the final trip home. He had a vision via his dead grandfather to seek his roots and overcame many obstacles to find them. Peter had indeed, in every therapeutic and archetypal sense, taken the Hero's Journey to the wholeness of his True Self.

CHAPTER XV

The Far Shore

Your journey through *The Dream Belongs to the Dreamer* is coming to an end. I sincerely hope you reach the far shore with confidence, a willingness to commit to dreamwork, and a much deeper understanding of your dreams. If you're still feeling challenged, that's OK. This is the kind of book meant to be at your side as a reference and a guide. Don't be shy about tossing it in your backpack, purse, briefcase, saddlebag, wherever. It was written as a reference guide, one you can refer to anytime the need arises.

If life calls and you're too busy to work on your dreams having it handy will also work as an instant refresher course. For example, you may want to go over the Subjective Symbol Immersion Method (SSIM) a few more times until you regain your mastery. Or put to memory, once and for all, the three guiding principles of dreamwork. If you recall they are:

1. The dream belongs to the dreamer.
2. Don't literalize the dream.
3. Don't moralize about dream content.

Perhaps learning more about Carl Jung and his many volumes of work on dreams and their meaning may call to you. There are countless free resources online or his nutshell quote on dreams may be enough. Remember Jung states, "The whole dreamwork is essentially subjective, and a dream is a theater in which the dreamer is himself the scene, the player, the prompter, the producer, the author, the public, and the critic." Jung's quote dovetails nicely with another one of our favorite theorists, Eugene Gendlin. Do you recall when Gendlin says Psyche is a house "where dreams come as guests through the unconscious. Welcome them as you would an invited guest. And trust the process." Sigmund Freud plays a role to a lesser degree not having looked beyond the Drive Theory with its emphasis on sexuality. This book is all about personal growth throughout one's lifetime.

Finally there is Gestalt Theory, this author's favorite fallback method that worked so well in Julia's dream. Remember her breakthrough when she became the white ringing phone? I hope you were inspired by her work to seek your primary symbol and explore it on the deepest level.

And who could forget the extraordinary and surprising revelation when Bill worked so hard to uncover his flaming redhead symbol in the thin white dress? Who would have imagined?

If you haven't worked on your dreams for a while, Chapter V, "To the Heart of Your Dream," will be a great first resource for you to begin to tackle them, especially if you have had a new and troubling or repetitive dream. There you'll find your guideposts and the beginning of your personal treasure map. It's the chapter with a workbook-like quality to it designed to get you writing and connecting the dots. This is also the chapter that encourages you to go deeper into the dream, to not settle for the obvious. It's challenging but oh so rewarding and life-affirming. Chapter VI follows with its detailed step-by-step guide to working with your primary dream symbol.

As you continue to use this book as a reference you'll find many definitions scattered throughout its pages. Some chapters rely heavily on them and in the back of the book they are organized in a tidy little reference guide for you. It's a good idea to have core definitions at your fingertips just in case you've left your book by the bedside. Core concepts and ideas, such as the primary symbol, Subjective Symbol Immersion Method (SSIM), archetypes, the Shadow, and the Hero's Journey, are great touchstones to ongoing dreamwork wherever you may be.

As your journey through *The Dream Belongs to the Dreamer* got more challenging and less obvious you were asked to step up and, just by being here reading it, you did. Congratulations. Julia's simple dream example morphed throughout the book into more and more challenging dream journeys, ones, like Amanda's vampire dream, that required professional help. Knowing when that need arises is also good to understand. Peter's hero journey might be another. It all depends on how much insight and personal work goes into it and let's not forget the synchronistic conversation he had with his sister that hit him hard, changed his thinking and started him on his Hero's Journey. Peter's dream of the map, as brief as it was, was a Big Dream, one that kept him invested in its outcome. Not everyone will feel the same way nor react as he did. In addition, we'll never know if any of these complicated dreams will, over time, transform into repetitive dreams and the dreamer will eventually be compelled to deal with it.

Chapter IX was an opportunity to rest and review your journey. A time to reset goals and possibly retrace some steps. With a process as powerful as the Subjective Symbol Immersion Method (SSIM) a pause and reflection can be very helpful and hopefully you found it an island of respite and reflection. We all need a break sometimes.

The remaining chapters were devoted to archetypes and their powerful presence in our daily lives. Those symbols in human form that are such a part of Jung's collective unconscious. Our primitive way of getting a grasp on the people around us once we venture forth into the world. Archetypes that resonate not only from the timeless unconscious but also from our very early environment. Archetypes such as Mother and Father in easily recognizable forms such as teachers and coaches who help us continue our life quest. Archetypes that by their very nature can be transgendered and often shaped by the societies and cultures we live in. In other words teachers can be men and coaches women, yet each can embody the Mother and Father primary archetype.

As promised very early in the book you have reached the far shore. It is time to disembark, taking with you all the tools in this book that will help you continue your life journey. Thanks for trusting me to be your helmsman and guide.

Velva Lee Heraty, aka Dream Momma

REFERENCE I:

What's Your Dream I.Q.?

(Tip: Remember to think about what something IS vs. what it DOES)

It's never a bad idea to test your knowledge in case you have to reinforce some ideas or terms. Here is a fun and brief self-test. Simply circle the number(s) you think is correct. The answers are at the end. Good luck!

1. SSIM stands for...
    1. Subjective Symbol Immersion Method.
    2. Seek, Search, Imagine and Mindfulness.
    3. Swinging Sisters in Manhattan.

2. At the heart of SSIM is...
    1. The Dream belongs to the Dreamer.
    2. Taking ownership of your dreams.
    3. Getting a soft and slow massage.

3. The first client to challenge the old dream method was...
    1. A flight attendant.
    2. A working mom.
    3. A disco dancer.

4. The difference between dream analysis and dream facilitation is...
    1. Analysis answers questions and facilitation asks them.
    2. Clients have input into the dream process.
    3. Vanilla and chocolate.

5. Temenos is...
    1. A town on the Aegean Sea coast.
    2. A sacred space.
    3. A Greek toga design.

6. The therapeutic relationship is bound by...
    1. Integrity
    2. Honesty
    3. Trust

7. A symbol is...
    1. A note on a musical scale.
    2. An object or person in a dream.
    3. Something that represents something else.

8. Write down the Three Guiding Principles of Dreamwork.
    1.____

    ____

    2.____

    ____

    3.____

    ____

9. Who said..."Dreams come as guests through the unconscious?"

1. Carl Jung
2. Eugene Gendlin.
3. Orson Wells.

10. Symbol interpretation books should be...

1. Banned.
2. Burned.
3. Shredded.

11. One of the things you should not do with a symbol is...

1. Judge it.
2. Literalize it.
3. Put it in a pipe and smoke it.

12. Carl Jung was a...

1. Swiss psychiatrist.
2. The father of analytical psychology.
3. Father of Sebastian Jung, the adventure writer.

13. In the Gestalt Method of DreamWork we...

1. Ask the dreamer to BE the symbol.
2. Understand that the elements are part of a whole.
3. Create a poem about our dream.

14. How many signposts are in Chapter V?

1. Ten.
2. Three.
3. Too many.

15. The Primary Symbol is...
    1. The thing or person that carries the most energy.
    2. The thing or person that stands out from all the others.
    3. The biggest thing in a dream.

16. When working on a dream the first question to ask yourself is...
    1. Where am I in the dream?
    2. How old am I in the dream?
    3. What's for dinner?

17. The Three Primary Selves are...
    1. Frightened, Fearless, and True
    2. Id, Ego and Super-Ego
    3. Curly, Moe, and Larry.

18. What does the ringing phone symbolize in Julia's dream?
    1. Her mother nagging her.
    2. Her role as the family switchboard.
    3. A bill collector.

19. The best way to look at a dream is to...
    1. View it as a play, movie, or story.
    2. Write it down and then read it.
    3. Through Dali's eyes.

20. Whose dream triggered a Hero's Journey?
    1. Bill.
    2. Peter.
    3. Tom.

21. Archetypes...
    1. Are models of people, behaviors, or personalities.
    2. Hang out in the Psyche.
    3. Influence our beliefs and decisions.

22. The Shadow...
    1. Represents the part of our psyche that is judged "bad" by us.
    2. A fragment of our primitive self.
    3. A Michael Jackson dance number.

23. The Persona...
    1. Is how we represent ourselves to the world.
    2. Appears in dreams.
    3. A new HBO series.

24. What popular movies have many archetypes in them?
    1. The Wizard of Oz.
    2. Breakfast Club.
    3. Conan the Barbarian.

25. Keeping a dream journal will...
    1. Help you remember your dreams.
    2. Identify recurring symbols.
    3. Identify themes in your dreams.

Answers:

1. 1. Subjective Symbol Immersion Method.

2. 1 & 2. The dream belongs to the dreamer and taking ownership of your dreams.

3. 1. A flight attendant.

4. 2. Clients have input into the dream process.

5. 2. A sacred space.

6. All. Integrity, Honesty, Trust.

7. 3. Something that represents something else.

8. The Dream belongs to the Dreamer.
   Don't literalize a dream.
   Don't moralize about dream content.

9. 2. Eugene Gendlin.

10. All. Banned, burned, shredded.

11. All. Judge it, literalize it, put it in a pipe and smoke it.

12. 1. & 2. Swiss psychiatrist and the father of Analytical Psychology.

13. 1. Ask the dreamer to BE the symbol.

14. 2. Three.

15. 1 & 2. The thing or person that carries the most energy and the thing that stands out from all the others.

16 2. How old am I in the dream?

17. 1. Frightened, Fearless, and True.

18. 2. Her role as the family switchboard.

19. 1. Viewing it as a play, movie or story.

20. 2. Peter.

21. 1. Models of people, behaviors, or personalities.

22. 1 & 2. Represents the part of our psyche that is judged "bad" by us and a fragment of our primitive self.

23. 1. How we present ourselves to the world.

24. 1 & 2. The Wizard of Oz and the Breakfast Club.

25. All. Help you remember your dreams, Identify themes in your dreams and Identify recurring symbols.

Your Score: ____________________

REFERENCE II

Glossary of Terms

Active Imagination: A technique that relies on the imagination to fully understand something, particularly something symbolic or abstract like dreams. The practice is found across all cultures. Jung believed it had great therapeutic value.

Anima: A term coined by Carl Jung to describe the unconscious feminine nature and energy of the male.

The Animus: A term coined by Carl Jung to describe the unconscious masculine nature and energy of the female.

Archetypes: Models of people, behaviors, or personalities. They can be classic, i.e. the Goddess, or modern, i.e. the Diva

Collective Unconscious: A term coined by Carl Jung and one of the core beliefs of his psychological theory. In essence he believes that we are all one with the universe. That we are all linked from the beginning of time to each other and other life force energies. The Collective Unconscious exists outside of our awareness and is global vs. the personal unconscious that is specific and unique to each person.

Dreams: Products of the unconscious mind acting involuntarily and spontaneously to bring psychic material to the conscious mind for processing.

Dream Facilitation: The process of moving through the steps and levels of dreamwork keeping focused on the symbols and the feelings and meanings of the symbols. Helping guide the Subjective Symbol Immersion process.

Dream Partnership: The process of dream facilitation that involves two people willing to guide one another through the various steps of dreamwork and the method of Subjective Symbol Immersion without personal interpretation or influence on the dreamer or the dream symbols.

The Eight Ages of Man: According to Developmental Psychologist Erik Erikson, there are eight psychological developmental stages each with it's own task of mastery necessary to go to the next stage with a firm foundation. They are condensed here. For the complete details read his book, *Childhood and Society.*

1. **Basic trust vs. basic mistrust** - This stage covers the period of infancy. 0-1 year of age. Successful in this, the baby develops a sense of trust, which "forms the basis in the child for a sense of identity."

2. **Autonomy vs. Shame** - 1-3 years of age. The beginning of mastering bodily functions. Self will appears.

3. **Initiative vs. Guilt** - Preschool, 3–5 years of age. A child's ability to do things on his or her own. The beginning of a sense of purpose.

4. **Industry vs. Inferiority**- School Age, 5-12. Child can recognize major differences in personal abilities relative to other children. Competency develops.

5. **Identity vs. Role Confusion** - Adolescent / 12 years till 18. The confusion and trials of coming of age in the quest for the True Self. True to oneself.

6. **Intimacy vs. isolation** - This is the first stage of adult development. This development usually happens during young adulthood, which is between the ages of 18 to 35. Work, career, and partnership choices are clear. Ability to love others.

7. **Generativity vs. stagnation**- The second stage of adulthood and happens between the ages of 35-64. The True Self gets grounded with a sense of purpose. Engaged in the family and community. Caring for others goes to the forefront.

8. **Ego integrity vs. despair**- This stage affects the age group of 65 and on. People, who have achieved what is important to them, look back on their lives and feel a sense of accomplishment. A time of mentorship. Wisdom.

Interpersonal: A level of dream processing that involves the subjective nature and response of the dreamer to dream symbols. The most "hands on" level of dream processing not requiring extensive knowledge of world religions, myths, fables or history. A level that can be applied immediately to one's life and to one's concerns, issues and conflicts.

Parental Introject: A part of the parent or primary caretaker(s) throughout childhood that becomes a fraction of the victim's psyche, like a splinter, infecting, to some degree, all other parts.

Personal Unconscious: Where we store all our individual suppressed memories, while the collective unconscious is a part of the psyche that functions on a larger scale. Jung looked at it as a container of psychological inheritance that contains all of the buried knowledge and experiences we share as being part of the human condition. Just think of it as a DNA of the mind.

Collective Unconscious: The collective unconscious, Jung believed, is where archetypes exist. He suggested that these models, in the classical sense, are innate, universal and hereditary. Archetypes such as Mother Earth, The Warrior, The Child, etc. are in our very nature and function to organize how we experience certain things. Other sub-archetypes such as the modern ones such as Nerd or Diva, mentioned earlier can be learned as they culturally develop and then become personally integrated.

Primary Symbol: The thing or person in a dream that carries the most energy. The thing or person the dreamer responds to most emotionally.

Self: The total of the coming together of all the unconscious and conscious elements of an individual. In other words, all parts of your psychological world.

Shadow: represents the part of our Self that is judged "bad" by us. Sometimes it isn't bad at all, but as children we were taught it was. The Shadow is also a fragment of our primitive self, the self whose only goals are sex and survival.

Symbol: The best possible expression for something unknown to the conscious Self.

> *"Every psychological expression is a symbol if we assume that it states or signifies something more and other than itself which eludes our present knowledge." (C. G. Jung).*

Jung distinguished between a symbol and a sign. Insignia on uniforms, for instance, are not symbols but signs that identify the wearer, unlike for example, a cardinal. In subjective interpretations a cardinal can be a priest, a baseball player, a color or a bird. It can also be a type of sin. It really does depend on what the individual associates it to.

Whether something is interpreted as a symbol or a sign depends mainly on the dreamer. Both are important but for the purpose of dreamwork facilitation and the Subjective Symbol Immersion Method we will be viewing symbols as representing *Something Unknown* to us at the time of the dream.

Subjective: Proceeding from or taking place within an individual's psyche (mind) and unaffected by the outside world. *Something unique experienced by a given individual.*

Subjective Symbol Immersion Method (SSIM): process means *protecting the symbol from external influences* by keeping the process within the individual psyche. This is very important and the biggest challenge of the dreamwork technique. In addition people tend to project their own personal meaning and interpretation onto the dreamer's symbol thus violating the dreamer's boundaries and not honoring the dreamers personal association. The reason it is important to stay on the subjective level is because the symbol represents a message that emerges and is within one part of the dreamer's unconscious to another, something like a phone call or note from a best friend, meant only for the dreamer and the dreamer alone. It is important to remember that the internal message delivered to someone's conscious mind through symbols is *always meant to help and always truthful.*

Temenos (Sacred Space) Jungians use the Greek word *temenos* to describe the sacred space of the therapeutic relationship. A relationship bound by integrity, honesty, trust and strong boundaries. The word can also be used to describe a safe container either real such as an urn for ashes or psychological represented by a core value and principles.

Three Cardinal Rules of DreamWork:

1. The dream belongs to the dreamer.
2. Don't literalize the dream. Dreams are symbolic, not literal.
3. Don't moralize a dream. Dreams are neither good nor bad, they just are.

Trancendent Function. The Transcendent Function is the part of your psyche that unites feelings and intellect to create a third and higher, experience. An experience that contributes to the ongoing formation of the True Self. It is pure and inexpressible. Think of joy. We can experience it but we can never articulate or fully describe it.

True Self: The person you were meant to be. Your authentic self. The Self without Personas (masks).

Types of Dreams

Pursuit Dreams
Quest Dreams
Journey Dreams
Shadow Dreams
House Dreams
Lost Dreams
Infant Dreams
Toddler Dreams
Child Dreams
Dark Stranger Dreams
Animal Dreams
Water Dreams
Flying Dreams
Falling Dreams
Sexual Dreams
Childhood Friend Dreams
Fighting Dreams (as with another person)
War Dreams
Pregnancy Dreams
Late for Dreams
Lost Love Dreams
Dreams of the Deceased
Others:

____

____

____

REFERENCE III

The Dreamer's Toolkit©

Forward:

In this section you will find helpful guidelines, techniques, tools and exercises, some mentioned in *The Dream Belongs to the Dreamer.* There are many bonus ones too. I've condensed them into a Dreamer's Toolkit for an easy reference. This will also help you view your dream from a variety of different angles. Finally, it's an opportunity to practice and acquire more knowledge and mastery of your dreams and the method of dreamwork.

Here are a number of successful methods and rituals that you may find useful as you work on your dreams. Some are simple and others complicated, but what they all have in common is that they work. As you progress you may find or create others that work as well. If you do, please share them with me so I can pass them along to others.

Trouble Remembering Your Dreams?
Try these Ideas

1. Take a personal interest in dreams.
2. Tell yourself every night right before bedtime that you WILL remember your dreams. Do this for at least a week or until you do remember a dream, even a dream fragment.
3. Read a non-clinical dream book (not a symbol book).
4. Browse the Internet to learn about dreams.
5. Start a dream journal. If you have one review it before bedtime.
6. Think about your most recent dream.
7. Don't move quickly upon awakening.
8. Keep a pen or pencil and paper, iPad or other recording device by your bedside.
9. Write your dream down immediately upon awakening. Even a dream fragment is important.
10. Circle keywords and symbols in the dream.
11. Write a brief story about your dream using who, what, where, when and how. The why will follow.
12. To increase REM sleep (Rapid Eye Movement-when we all dream) drink a large glass of water right before bedtime.

Find the Primary Symbol

The primary symbol is *the thing or person that has the most energy for you.* The thing or person in the dream you *emotionally respond to the most.* The one object or person that keeps coming back to you as you think about the dream. It can be anything,

anything at all but it *can be only one.* Remember too that if it is a person, the person is symbolic, not literal. In other words, if it's your boss, he or she probably represents authority.

Remember The Three Guiding Principals

1. The dream belongs to the dreamer.
2. Don't literalize a dream.
3. Don't moralize about dream content.

Use Your Signpost Material

Get a clean piece of paper and rewrite the dream. Go over it and circle or underline the parts of the dream that you can group under the three Signpost categories; Finding the primary symbol, understanding it, and connecting it. Remember, not everything will fit neatly into these categories but recognize the ones that do. Keep at it. This will be the core of all your dreamwork.

Create a Sacred Space (Temenos)

First, gather four primary stones no larger than a baby's fist or golf ball. You can mark these stones North, South, East and West after determining the directions from your location. Next, place the four primary stones facing their proper directions making sure they are far enough apart for you to write while you sit inside the circle. Once your directions are determined fill in the rest of the circle with smaller stones, once again making sure you can comfortably fit inside the circle. You can also place the stones around your desk or writing area at home if that works for you.

Understand that your temenos needn't be a permanent sacred space as the stones can be removed and placed in other areas as you see fit. *The idea is that the space within the circle of stones is sacred* no matter where you build your temenos. Step inside and sit down. If it doesn't feel right, do it again in another location until your felt-sense tells you your sacred space is in the right spot. Some of my clients who travel for a living carry their temenos stones in a pouch or box so they are right on hand. Other clients have purchased white sage and used it in a cleansing ritual after their circle was complete. Whatever works.

BE the symbol

Remember that in Gestalt symbolism we become the symbol in the dream. We use our imagination to become the physical aspects of the object. For example we dream of a shoe. We can imagine what a shoe must feel like having a foot enter it. Depending on the shoe we can imagine what a shoe must feel like being laced up tightly or what it must feel like stepping in a deep puddle or cold water or on big stones or broken, crunchy glass. Choose a primary symbol from one of your dreams and using your imagination write about **being** the symbol.

Do The Inner Child Exercise

Sit down, close your eyes and see your young self. If you're having trouble doing that dig up some old family or school pictures. What is the look on your face? Sad? Smiling? Write that down. Next check out your haircut, clothes and shoes. What are you wearing? Get very detailed here, i.e. socks? Also, remembering Gendlin's felt-sense with all its nuances, such as posture or position. Do you have downcast eyes? Are you sitting, standing, or slumping? Perhaps you are holding something or there is a toy or pet at your feet. The more details the better. Once you have a clear picture of your Inner Child, adopt him or her. Yes, adopt. Be a good parent and give your Inner Child all the love and support you can. Be sure to reassure him or her than you will not abandon or banish (reject) them. As an added bonus start a dialogue journal between yourself (as parent) and your Inner Child for a deeper connection and healing. Finally, don't freak out if he or she is deeply wounded. You made it didn't you? Keep remembering that.

Do The Radiating Exercise

Draw a circle in the center of a clean piece of paper. Write or draw your primary symbol in the middle of the circle. Focus on it until you start making connections to it. For each connection draw a line out from the circle (like a spoke) and write down the thing or experience you are reminded of. Do this until you get that Aha! moment or felt-sense as you are connecting the dots. Take a second piece of clean paper and do that again with the thing or experience you are reminded of until it comes full circle back to your primary symbol. Write about what you've learned.

Start a Dream Journal

Keeping a dream journal will be very rewarding over time. Write everything you remember about a dream in it, including fragments. DON'T edit the journal just keep writing for a few months. Then read the journal from the beginning paying attention to any themes, symbols, actions, or other things that occur *more than once.* This includes how you feel about the dream upon awakening.

Start a Feeling Journal

Many people distance themselves from their childhood memories. They either go into denial about them or experience them as so painful they refuse to deal with them. Either way our troubled past haunts us and often, when we're emotionally ready, the first ghostly memory of it appears in a dream. Now, on the first page of your feeling journal write these five words. Mad, Glad, Scared, Sad and Bad. These will be your touchstone words until you get comfortable with *all* your feelings and can begin to nuance or shade them For example, Mad can range from Rageful to miffed. Glad can be ecstatic all the way through to pleased. Remember your feelings define your True Self. They shape your world. If you are sitting on a pile of unexpressed feelings they will pop up somewhere, usually at the worst possible time, and when you least expect them.

Start a Dream Circle

Dream circles can be wonderful and supportive ways to work on your dreams. Use the three guiding principles as a framework for your circle. You will need at least four people but no more than eight. The thing most important about any group that gathers is that they stay *true to their purpose and all participants agree to and follow the same rules.* Here are ten basic guidelines to get you started. They are *all-important* and have at their core the idea of the dream circle being a sacred space or temenos.

1. Commit to a vow of confidentiality.
2. Meet once a week always on the same day and time. *No exceptions.*
3. Commit to be there regularly.
4. Start and end on time. (This is very therapeutic for everyone.)
5. Don't go longer than 1.5 hours.

6. Meet for at least eight weeks, on the seventh week decide if you want to continue.
7. No interpreting another's dream.
8. No cross talk.
9. Everybody contributes.
10. Celebrate on the last night.

Find a Dream Partner

Dream Partnership: The process of dream facilitation that involves two people willing to guide one another through the various steps of dreamwork and the method of Subjective Symbol Immersion without personal interpretation or influence on the dreamer or the dream symbols.

Create a Dream Board

Turn your dream into visual reality. Create a dream board in this easy two-step process that will allow you to visualize your dream and use your imagination to explore it. Making a dream board is a process, not an event, so take your time.

1. Gather poster board, glue sticks, glue guns, magazines, pictures, scissors and anything else you think will help you. Also, make a trip to the store and gather some additional items that remind you of your dream. Anything that is small and light enough to glue onto your poster board with a glue stick or glue gun will be fine.

2. Create a temenos (sacred space), set the mood, and do whatever helps you get in touch with your creative self. Then search through the items you have gathered and start posting them, in whatever order you want, to the board. As you work pay attention to what connects to what and write things down

as you experience them. Journal about what you're learning about the dream and more importantly what you're learning about yourself. (Suggested by Rebecca Bales)

Write a Short Story

Think of yourself as a writer who has to produce a short story using the material from the dream. Ask yourself who is in the dream? Where and when is the dream-taking place and what is the action? Finally ask yourself why. Why am I having this dream now? If the dream ends abruptly use your imagination to finish your dream story. If you are a skilled writer feel free to use other written mediums to process your dream such as novels, poetry, screen plays, etc.

Be an Artist

Allow your Inner Artist to merge. Sketch, draw, paint or sculpt your dream's primary symbol. You can do a collage or combine this exercise with creating a Dream Board. If your Inner Artist is a dancer or performance artist then dance or act out your dream. Follow with a feeling journal.

Advanced Dreamwork

Caution, if you are fragile in any way or inexperienced in dream methodology

DO NOT do the following three exercises alone. I'm Serious.

Do the Cover Art Exercise: Advanced Dreamwork

Study this image. Imagine your inner world represents the house. Note there are four primary waves threatening to engulf the house and one smaller one on the lower right. There are also two waves that are out of the image but indicated by water to the left and right near the bottom of the house. That's five visible waves and two implied ones for a total of seven waves. Pay attention to the largest wave first. Study it, think about it, and sleep on it. Then write down who or what it represents. Do the same with each of the other three larger waves. Do you see a theme? Are there dots you can connect? If the waves were inside of you psyche how can you calm or master them so your inner world is more manageable? Write all of this down.

Use Active Imagination: Advanced dreamwork.

Active Imagination is a method or way of studying your dreams, dream state, dream behavior and anything else related to your dreaming world. For our purposes the technique is best used going back to a dream that challenges you, puzzles you, and *ends abruptly*. First, go to your temenos (safe place) and lie down. Relax and clear your mind. If you've recorded the dream read it over, perhaps more than once to get a firm grasp of its details, then close your eyes and go back to the unfinished dream. Next, remembering that anything is possible, try to *imagine* how the dream ends. If you're feeling challenged, go back, tap into your creativity again, and *reimagine* what happened right after the dream ended abruptly and you woke up. Do this a number of times until your felt-sense tells you what feels right. Be prepared for shadow material to emerge. Remember your unconscious and your defense structure will not send you material that will overwhelm you. If you get frightened trust yourself to handle it.

Take a Vision Quest: Advanced Dreamwork

A Vision Quest is a Native American rite of passage where the male youth of the tribe undergo a challenging ritual designed both as a separation from boyhood and to determine the new role the youth will have in the tribe. Fasting and surviving the wilderness for weeks at a time is intended to bring on the vision. It is believed that the vision and the wilderness experience prophesize the youth's future. For example, if the young man outruns a deer in his vision he may be named Outruns a Deer and given the role of a hunter or advanced scout. To make this work best for you in today's world, take the bones of a vision quest and design your own journey. For example, do something that involves, travel, the wilderness, challenges, and fasting. Outward Bound would be a good contemporary choice. The only thing I recommend is sharing your intentions with someone you can trust, make sure you have an emergency plan, and adding two days at the end of your personal vision quest for introspection and journaling.

REFERENCE IV

Dream Momma's Art Gallery

A wonderful juried art exhibit called "Dreams" opened in St. Petersburg, FL on November 2, 2013. The following images are black and white versions of thirteen artistic renderings of the subject that were in the show. You can see the full color originals at www.dreammomma.com

Dive by Dennis Ramos. dramos2@gmail.com

Queen of the Night by Shawn Bowen,
obishawnkenobi@hotmail.com

Journeys by Nikki Emmons, swtannmrie@yahoo.com

Swift Creek by Fred Spinks, artistdorian@hotmail.com

Dream Time by Boo Ehrsam, boosart@tampabay.rr.com

Waiting for Love to Drop by Kevin Von Holtermann, kev.von.holt@gmail.com

The Lovers by Steven Kenny, info@stevenkenny.com

The Artist's Dream by Cathy Lees, kreativekat47@gmail.com

Anxiety by Rebekah Eugenia Lazaridis, redlazaridis@gmail.com

Becoming a Rose by Mirella Cimato,
mirella.cimato@gmail.com

The Hero's Dream Battle with the Shadow
by Karan Porter, karanporter@verizon.com

Fall Forward by Brandon Scott,
brandonscottartworks@gmail.com

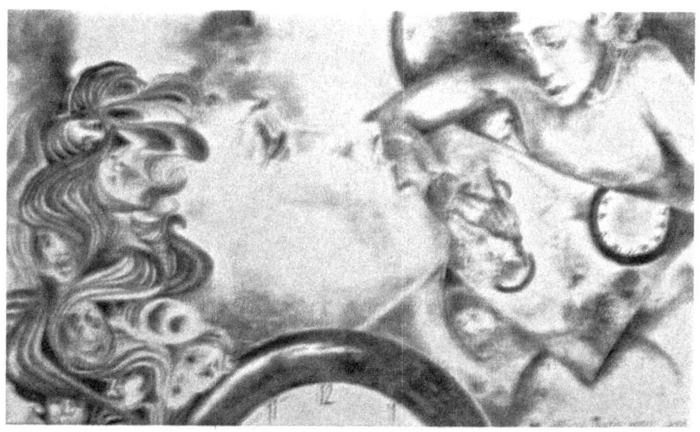

Dream Labyrinth by Patricia Warren, pw081251@aol.com

ABOUT THE COVER ARTIST

Rebekah Eugenia Lazaridis is a painter from St. Petersburg, FL, USA. She received her Bachelor of Fine Arts (BFA) from The School of The Art Institute of Chicago and apprenticed for USA 829 for Scenic Painting in New York City. She has painted professionally for nearly eight years and has worked on various film, TV series, and Broadway plays as well as local theater productions. Her personal work focuses on dramatic and emotional images, symbolic themes and archetypes as well as illustrative and often whimsical characters. www.RebekahLazaridis.com

WITH DEEPEST GRATITUDE

My little ship, with its steadfast passengers, could never have gotten to the far shore without the help of my talented advisors and friends. We've had quite a journey together. My deepest gratitude to Nancy Wisenfeld a friend, ace editor, and critical thinker who sat in NY for weeks poring over every word of my final draft. Nancy you are terrific and you gave me the confidence I needed to submit my manuscript. Stephen Danzig, from across the pond, worked his magic throughout this challenging journey. His talent, media skills, insight and feedback were always on course. Steve, you are amazing and I am so lucky to benefit from your generous spirit. Michael Ritchie, a web design whiz was onboard from the beginning. We planned a website three years ago when I began my marathon revisions and he held the course throughout. I'm so grateful for his talent and loyalty. Thank you so much Michael! You totally rock.

As I write this gratitude letter I flashback to 2008 when my daughter Quinn, after learning I had been teaching my SSIM theory across the globe, raised an eyebrow. She suggested I write a book about my method before an enterprising trainee did. I raised both eyebrows and began to plan that very thing. Later, when I was deciding how to move forward, she mentioned five great reads on the current publishing industry that helped me make one of my biggest decisions ...how to publish. Thanks Q!

A deep heartfelt thanks to the very first special engine that got this book out of my head and onto the page four years ago. This marvelous team held my hand while I took those baby-writing first steps. My deepest gratitude to Coach Simone Peer and her ace team, especially Adrian McGinn. Their input and support in the beginning carried me through my fear and resistance. That was huge for me. You have my heartfelt appreciation. Conor Hughes, my South African mentor, was instrumental in helping me structure *The Dream Belongs to the Dreamer* in its adolescence and I am eternally grateful for her keeping me on track. Without all of you I never would have gotten off the writing ground and into publication.

Wally Reule, my life long friend from Sedona, AZ offered me a writer's den among the red rocks and the first half of *The Dream Belongs to the Dreamer* was written in that spiritual temenos. He was a steadfast critical reader too. Wally, my gratitude is endless. The following summer, off I went to a farmhouse in Hanover Il, America's Heartland, courtesy of Chris Bell, where the second half of my book struggled out of my head and onto the page.

In addition an ocean of gratitude to Diane Craig, Cynthia Brennan, Jayne Zampelli, Michelle Sanchez, Rebecca Bales, Chris Lueders, Erik Remmel, Julie Larson, Michael Heraty, Tina Fischer, Susan Frasier, Steve Batten, Julia Sportolari, Maureen Surak, Rosemary Jansen Zelazek, Sherry Catrell Williamson, and Rebecca Long Purington, my go-to supporters for all those pesky little details that often ground my writing to a halt. They never failed to get me unstuck. Thank you all from the bottom of my heart.

Finally, to my little buddy Miss Nena, who sat faithfully at my feet keeping my loneliness at bay during every word of this incredible and challenging journey.

Velva Lee Heraty, AKA Dream Momma

- To order additional copies of *The Dream Belongs to the Dreamer* or to be on Dream Momma's e-mail and/or to read her blog go to www.dreammomma.com
- Have comments and feedback? E-mail the author at vlheraty@dreammomma.com
- Was *The Dream Belongs to the Dreamer* helpful? If so, please write a brief review on Amazon.com. It would mean a lot to me.
- On Facebook? Please "like" Dream Momma and visit often for regular postings. Thanks!
- The author hosts a weekly radio show called "Let's Talk Life!" Saturday mornings at 10:00 est. Go to www.lifeimprovementradio.com to listen live.
- All Dreamers welcome!

Printed in the United States
by Baker & Taylor Publisher Services